THE *Ninety Prettiest* COUNTY COURTHOUSES IN TEXAS...

AND THE TEN UGLIEST

by Kevin Miller

courthousebook.com

Copyright © 2023 Kevin Miller
ISBN 979-8-218-17247-3
First edition, 2023
Design and photographs by Kevin Miller – Additional credits on pp. 136–137

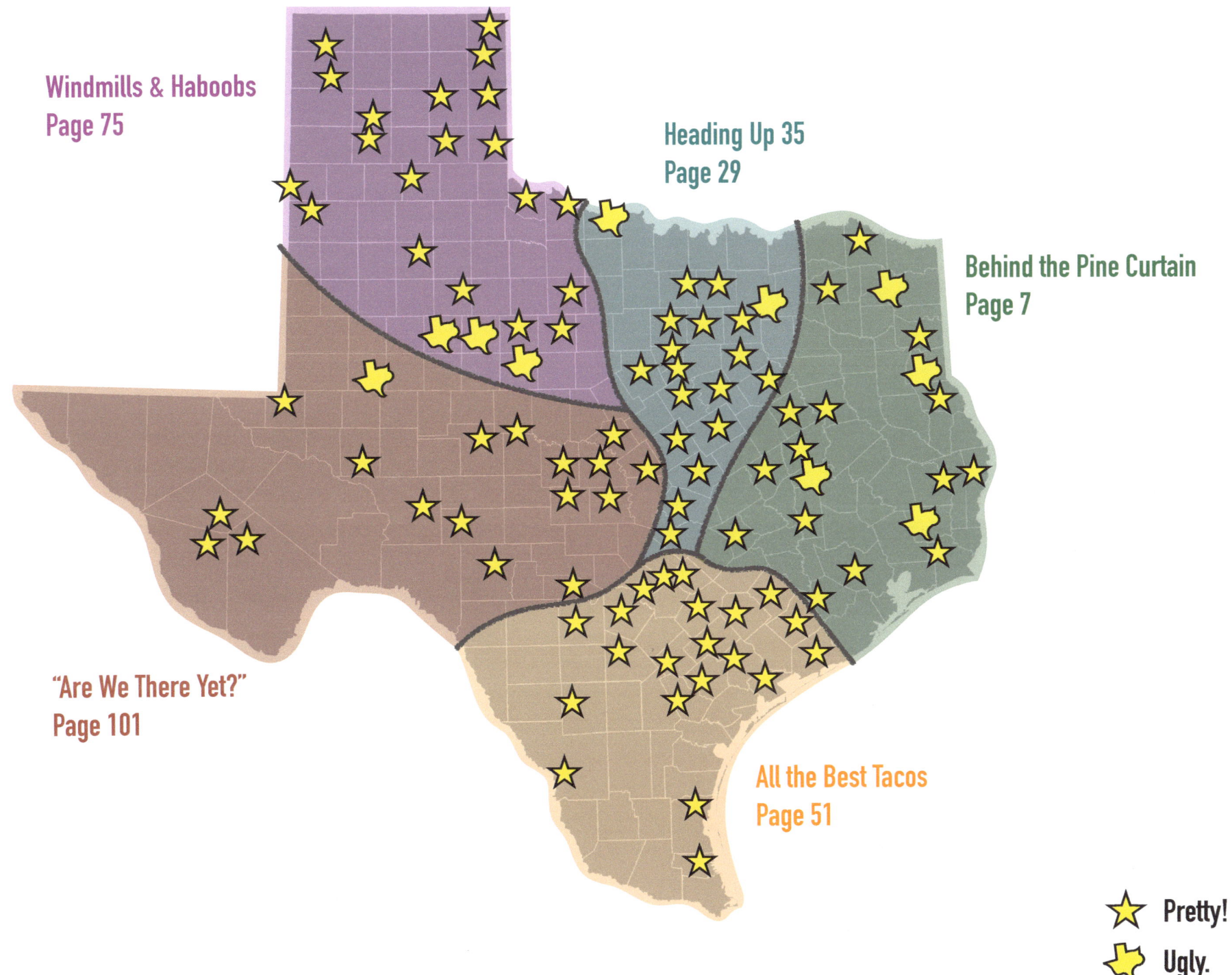

Windmills & Haboobs
Page 75

Heading Up 35
Page 29

Behind the Pine Curtain
Page 7

"Are We There Yet?"
Page 101

All the Best Tacos
Page 51

Pretty!

Ugly.

THIS HAS BEEN DONE BEFORE.

There are websites with more detail and books with better pictures. There's a $15 poster, perfect for your office wall. Back in the '90s, somebody made and sold tiny collectible ceramic models of Texas county courthouses. My friend and I found them at a department store and snickered at how kitschy they were. Twenty-five years later, here I am, assembling a kitschy coffee-table book on the same subject. Who's snickering now?

The origin story for this project is short. On a 2014 drive from Austin to Denver and back, my friend David Lampe and I entertained ourselves by stopping at county courthouses as we passed them and (beginning with Hartley County Courthouse in Channing, page 84) taking pictures. "Wouldn't it be fun," the conversation went, "if someone visited every county courthouse?" Fun might not be the word some would use, but that's exactly what I did.

At first I took pictures of courthouses as I happened to pass them by. Before long, I was making detours and day trips. In December 2020, a week before moving from Texas to The Netherlands, I visited the last few dozen in a single four-day journey. Why? Because I love road trips, I love old buildings, and—despite its considerable flaws—I love the state of Texas. Taking a single picture of the courthouse in each of our 254 counties, accruing unknown thousands of miles, was a decent way to scratch all of those itches. Even if only for a few minutes, I passed through almost every corner of this enormous state, visiting places I'd never seen before and never will again.

My feelings about the project evolved over the years. I was interested in these courthouses for their aesthetic value, but anybody who's taken half a history course knows that beautiful architecture can be a facade for some awful human behavior. These courthouses represent the places they inhabit, but they also represent a justice system that doesn't treat its citizens as equally as the blindfold would suggest. In short, I don't want to glorify the buildings without noting the times that they've failed the people they're supposed to serve.

Why feature only a hundred courthouses? Well, even if all of my 254 courthouse pics were worthy of print (they very much aren't), the middle 60% range from "pleasantly forgettable" to "crushingly dull." Even among the courthouses that I did select, there are a surprising number of twins and triplets—and one set of quadruplets!

When you're dealing with 254 of anything, you can expect some flux. Not long after I visited it, Fannin County Courthouse was restored to its former glory. Travis County recently replaced its Art Deco masterpiece with a glorified office building. The 1914 courthouse in Corpus Christi sits abandoned and forlorn, awaiting either restoration or destruction. Hell, Mason County Courthouse burned to the ground while I was designing this book! What I'm saying is, we'll surely need a second edition.

And if you're wondering about the architectural expertise that qualifies me for this project, then wonder no further: I have none! For this reason and others, I haven't ranked them—just picking a hundred was challenge enough. The pretty ones are largely from the "golden era" around the 1890s, though a few more recent buildings made the cut. The ugly ones are mostly minimum-budget boxes built or "renovated" around mid-century. In either case, I can claim no precise methodology. The buildings simply spoke to me. And what they said was: "Put me in your book."

One final caveat. Many many times, lovely old courthouses have been replaced by ugly newer ones but mercifully spared the wrecking ball. Sometimes the new one was so ugly I had to highlight it. Other times the old one was too pretty not to include. When you make a book, you make judgment calls.

On to the pretty pictures! Without further ado: ninety beautiful Texas courthouses, and—waiting for you every few pages, like cow patties in the bluebonnets—ten offensively ugly ones.

Kevin Miller, 2023

BEHIND THE PINE CURTAIN

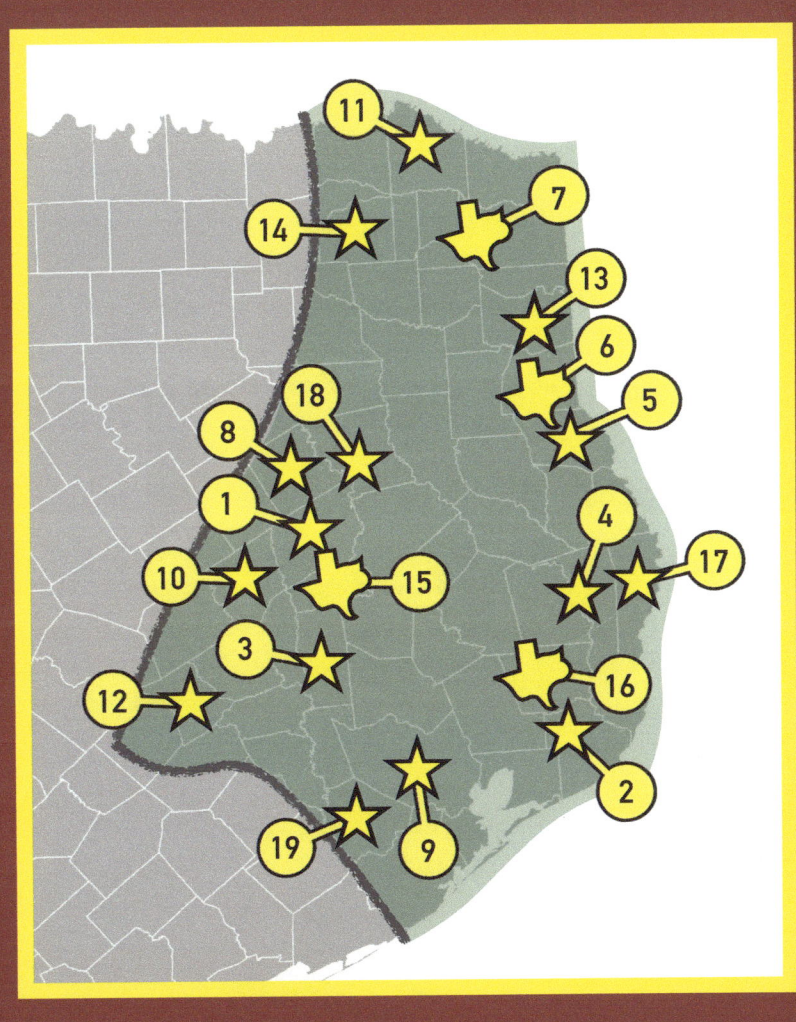

Leon County Courthouse

Centerville • 1886 • Restored 2007
Architect: William Johnson

After the 1858 courthouse burned down. Leon County built the new one on the same foundation using the same bricks. A 2007 restoration added modern touches—like bathrooms.

Jefferson County Courthouse

Beaumont • 1931
Architects: Fred C. Stone & A. Babin

Early in the Great Depression, Jefferson County thumbed its oil-stained nose at the stock markets and built one of Texas's few skyscraper courthouses. It's still the fifth-tallest building in town.

Also in downtown Beaumont, for reasons unclear: a Thomas Edison museum. (No, Thomas Edison never went to Beaumont.)

JEFFERSON COUNTY
COURT HOUSE

Grimes County Courthouse

Anderson • 1893 • Restored 2002
Architects: F.S. Glover and Co.

This is the fifth courthouse to be built for Grimes County after the previous four all burned down. (I think this was a Monty Python bit.)

ONE WAY →

Jasper County Courthouse

Jasper • 1889 • Expanded 1934
Architect: W.R. Kaufman

The cardboard-box-lookin' additions from 1934 are a points deduction, and the courtroom is a highlight, but the janitor's closet inside the safe is the real gem.

11

Shelby County Courthouse

Center • 1885

Architect: John J. E. Gibson

This building's architectural quirks include an escape hatch from the judge's bench down a hidden stairway.

5

Panola County Courthouse

Carthage • 1953
Architect: Preston M. Geren

This building's architectural quirks include a passing resemblance to a Cylon from Battlestar Galactica.

6

PANOLA COUNTY

UGLY!

Courtesy courthousehistory.com

Its 1885 predecessor was Shelby County's twin.

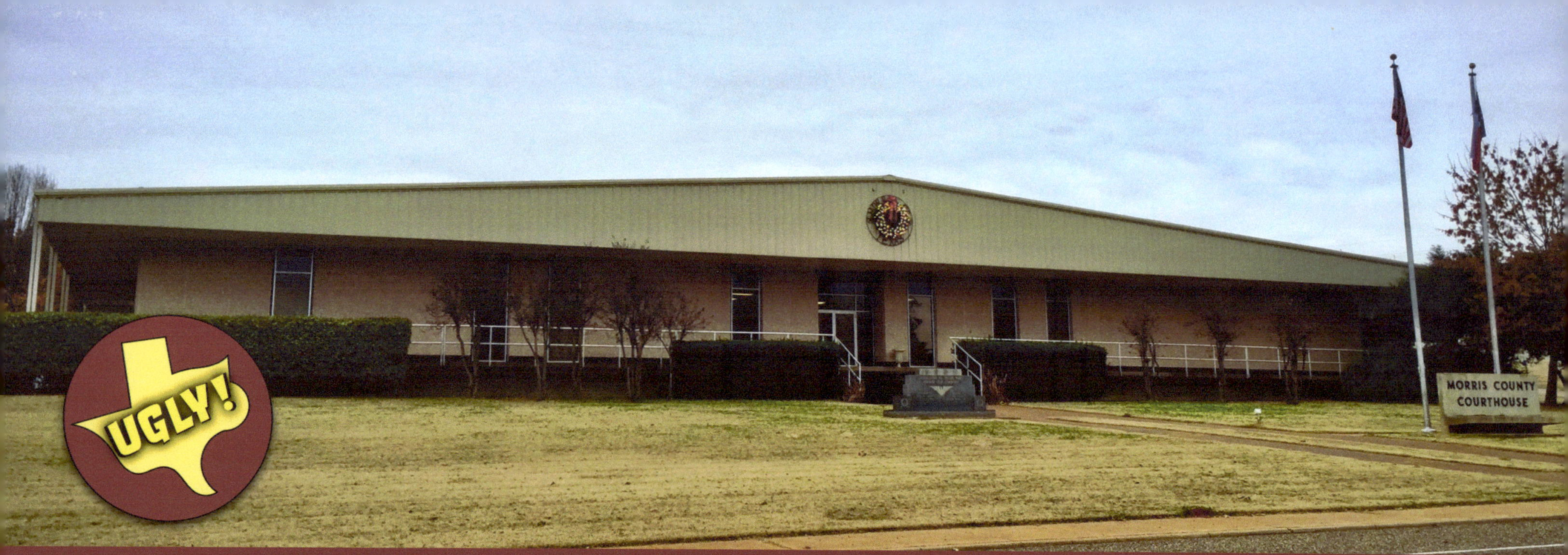

UGLY!

Morris County Courthouse

Daingerfield • 1973
Architects: Pierce, Pace, & Associates

The decorative Christmas wreath hardly even qualifies as lipstick for this pig of a courthouse. Luckily, there was a much more memorable building directly across the road: the Kissin' Kousins Kountry Kafe.

Kissin' Kousins
Kountry Kafe
Voted Best Chicken Fried Steak
& Best Home Cooking
903-645-7956
Sandwiches·Grilled Hamburgers

OPEN

STEAK

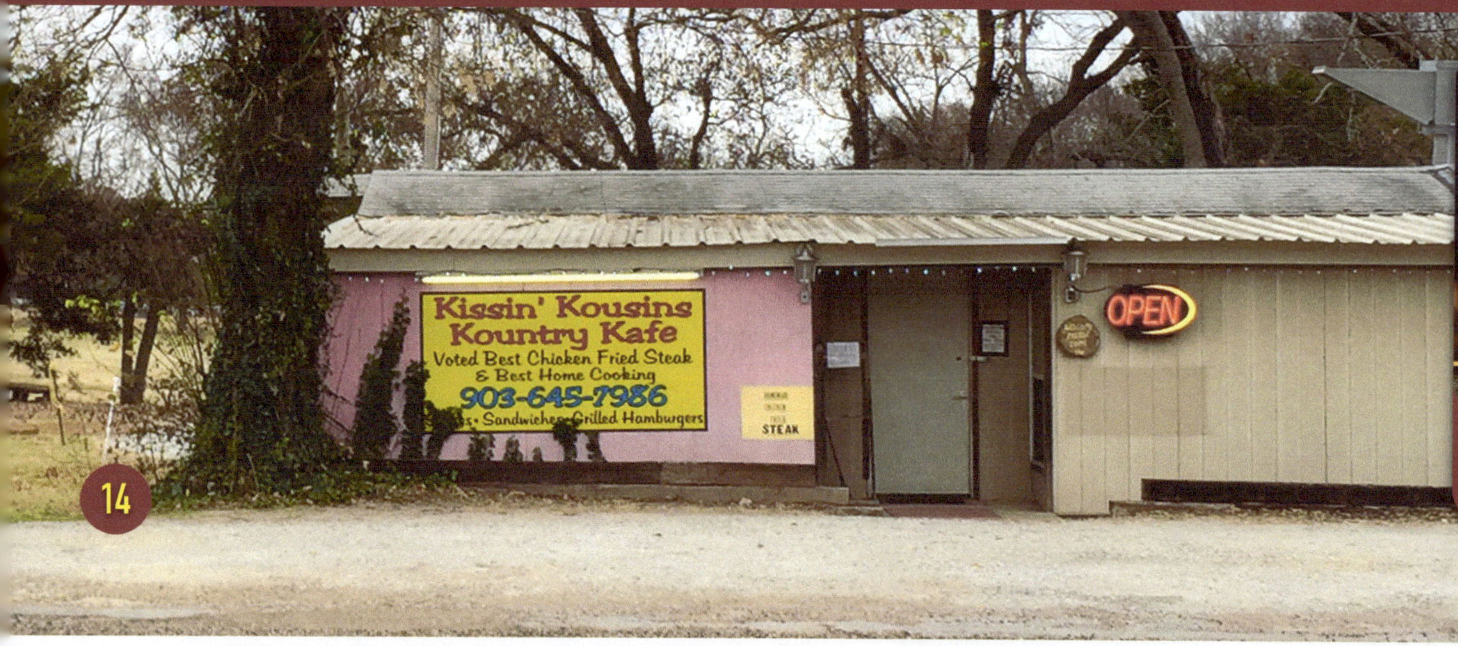

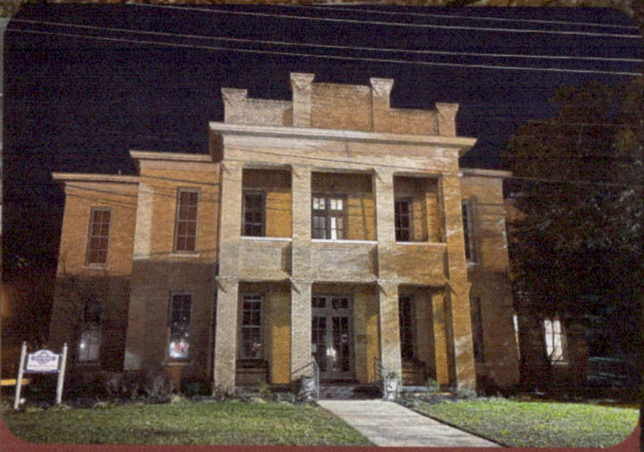

The 1882 courthouse stands nearby, wishing the 1970s never happened. (Don't we all.)

14

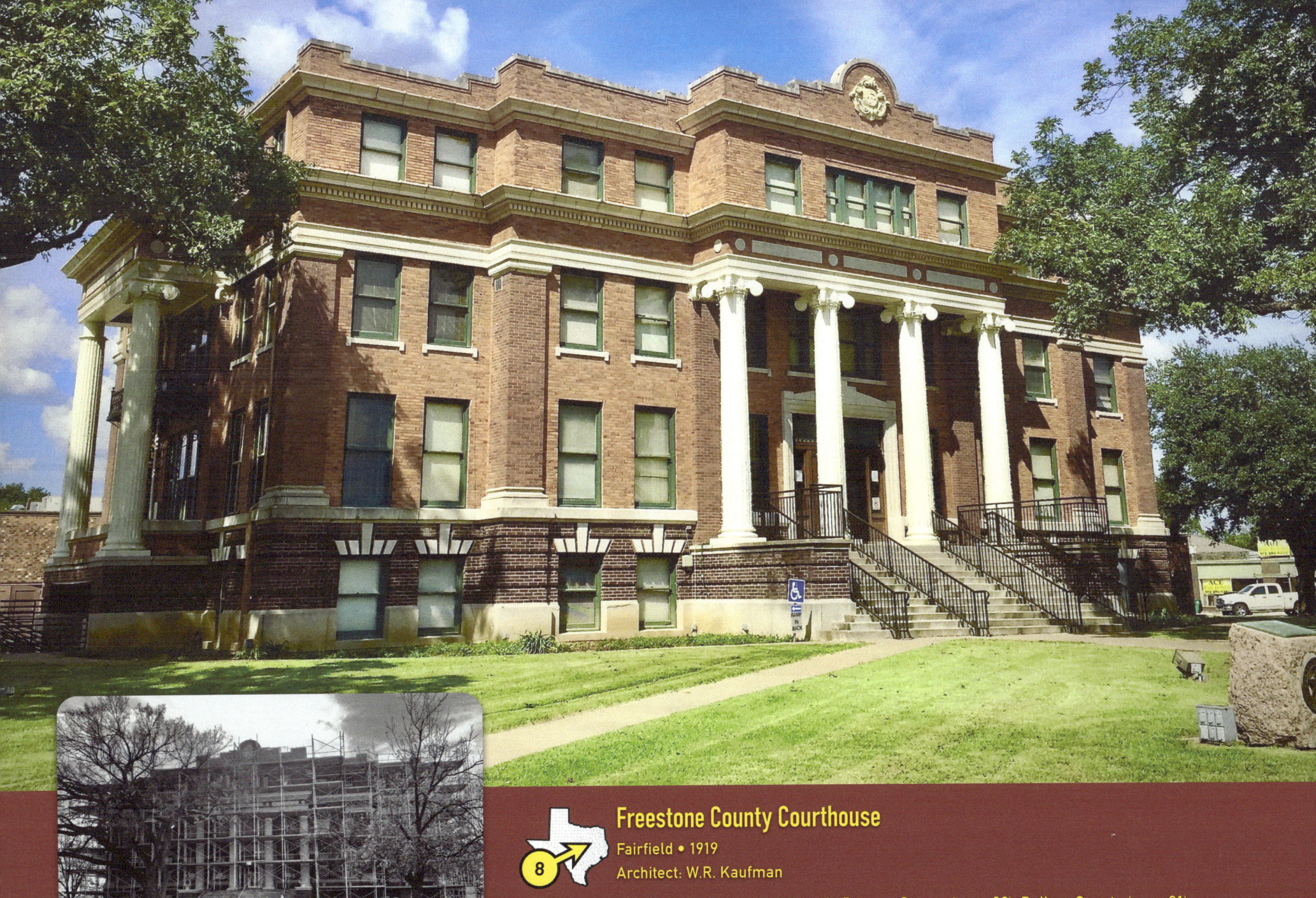

Freestone County Courthouse

Fairfield • 1919
Architect: W.R. Kaufman

This courthouse has near-identical siblings in Parmer County (page 80), Dallam County (page 81), and Lynn County (at left, mid-restoration when I visited in 2018). Here's what's really wild: all four courthouses have different credited architects. Who copied whose homework?

8

Harris County Courthouse

9

Houston • 1910 • Restored 2011
Architects: Lang, Witchell, & Barglebaugh

The modernist weirdos sapped the soul of Harris County
Courthouse when they "renovated" it in the 1950s. It cost
a cool $65 million to undo the damage and restore the
building fifty years later.

Try saying "Barglebaugh" five times fast.

Robertson County Courthouse

Franklin • 1883 • Restored 2014
Architect: Frederick Ernst Ruffini

Robertson County has been through four courthouses but _five_ county seats since its founding. I can't even decide on my pizza toppings, so I get it.

Red River County Courthouse

Clarksville • 1884 • Restored 2002
Architect: William H. Wilson

Late one night in 1961, the courthouse clock began chiming and rang more than 120 times before somebody finally pulled the plug. I guess there are perks to keeping your courthouse tower clock-free, as you'll see many counties have done.

Lee County Courthouse

Giddings • 1899 • Restored 2004
Architect: J. Riely Gordon

One of 15 Texas courthouses by James Riely Gordon, a Virginian with no formal architectural training. 12 of them are still standing, and 11 appear in this book. (Fayette County didn't quite make the cut, if you're wondering.)

This courthouse finished a restoration project in 2004, but when I visited a decade later, there were…umm…problems apparent. (I've read that the foundation has since been repaired.)

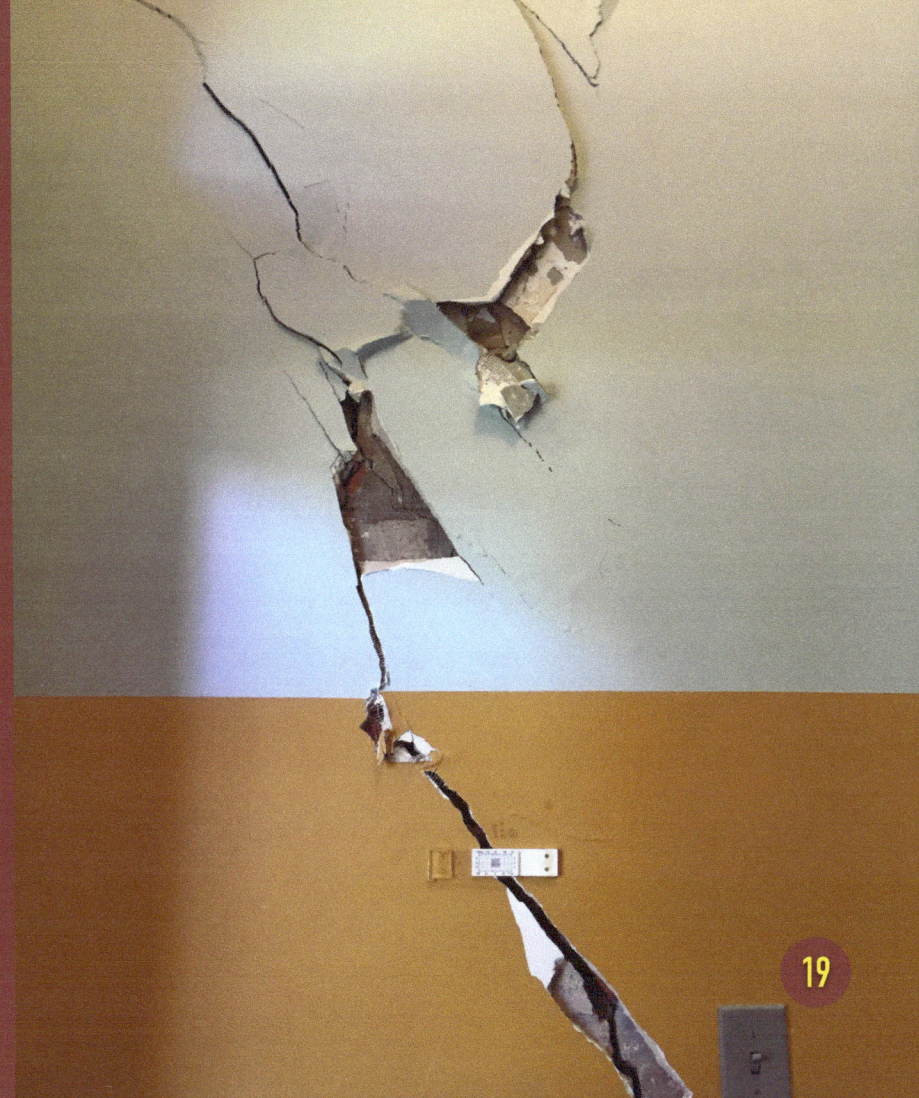

Harrison County Courthouse

Marshall • 1900 • Restored 2009
Architect: J. Riely Gordon

This imposing building dominates the Marshall town square like a battleship in a kiddie pool. It was functionally replaced by a nondescript box in 1964, but lives on as the Harrison County Historical Museum.

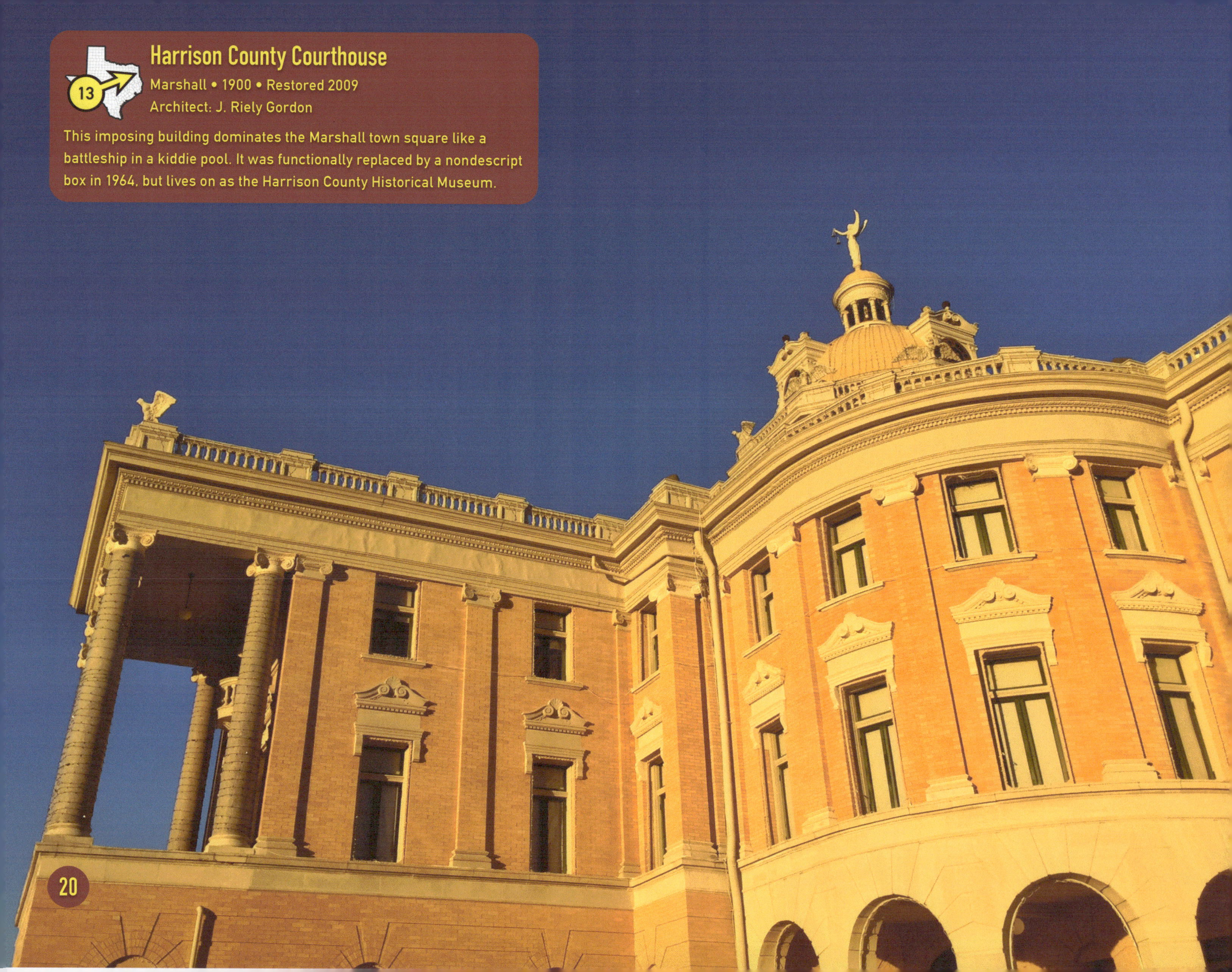

Hopkins County Courthouse

Sulphur Springs • 1895 • Restored 2002
Architect: J. Riely Gordon

14

Hopkins County Commissioner R. Carpenter had this to say when a clock was proposed for the tower: "Get up at sunup, go to bed at dark, eat when you are hungry, and you don't need no damn clock."

Sheesh, more like R. Grumpypants, am I right?

15 Texas

Madison County Courthouse

Madisonville • 1970

Architects: Dickson, Dickson, Buckley, & Bullock

Somebody ask the Fisher-Price Little People what the hell happened here. (And yes, of <u>course</u> the previous courthouse was fantastic.)

MADISON COUNTY COURTHOUSE

Courtesty TxDOT

UGLY!

UGLY!

Hardin County Courthouse

Kountze • 1958

Architects: Dickson, Dickson, & Associates

The Dicksons strike again. I might find something nice to say about Kountze's mid-century rectangle if it weren't displaying the top of its 1905 predecessor like a French king's disembodied head.

Fun fact: neither of those clocks was accurate.

Court House, Hardin Co., Tex.

Courtesy courthousehistory.com

23

Newton County Courthouse

Newton • 1903 • Restored 2012
Architects: Martin & Moodie

An electrical fire in 2000 completely gutted the original courthouse. It took six years for restoration work to begin, and another six years before it was finished. That's about how long it took me to make a dang picture book, so I can't really judge.

Smart.

Anderson County Courthouse

18

Palestine • 1914 • Renovated 1986
Architect: C.H. Page & Brother

Love the silver dome. Hate the Ugly Texas that somebody painted on the floor of the rotunda. (Seriously, just trace it.)

Charles and Louis Page designed seven Texas county courthouses. Four of them appear in this book, and two (this guy and Hays County, page 68) are nearly twins. Got any feedback? The firm is still in business!

HEADING UP 35

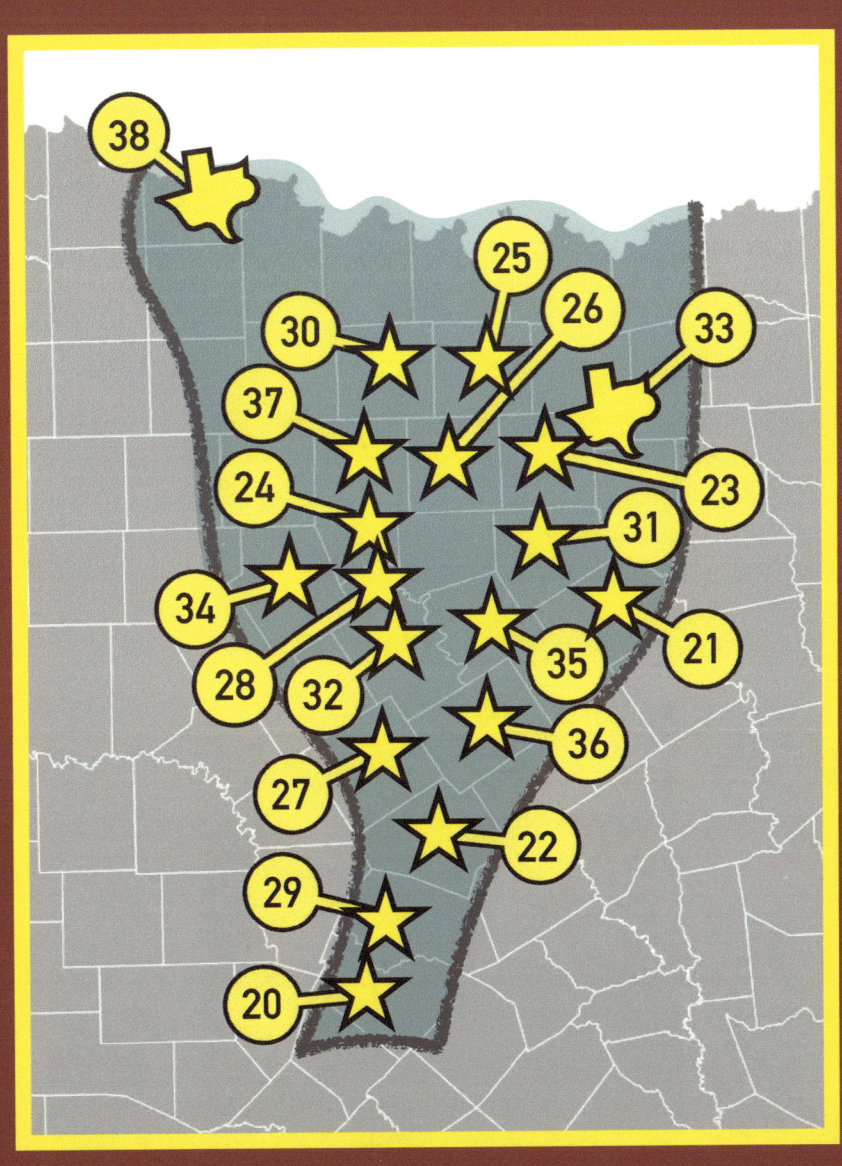

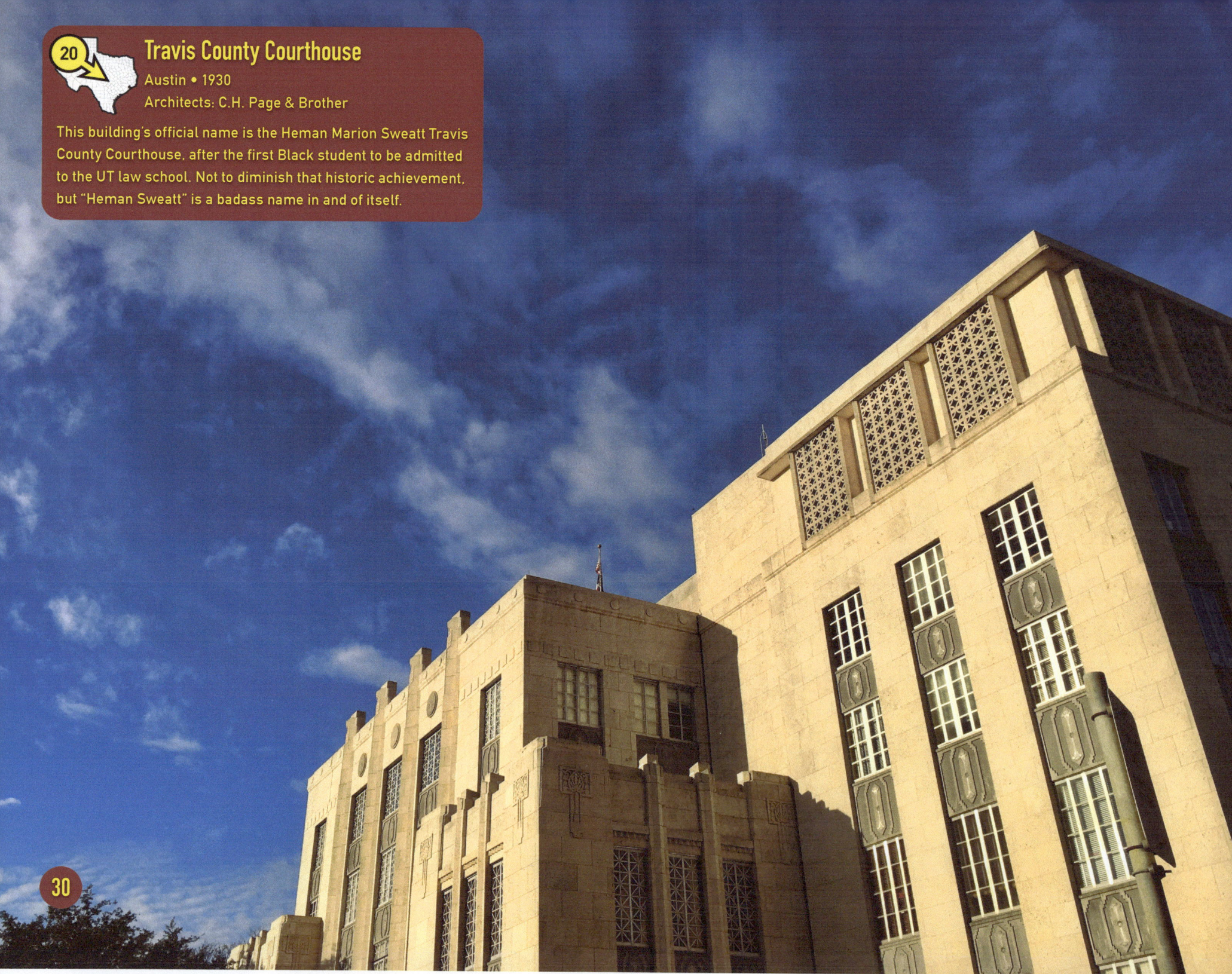

Travis County Courthouse

20

Austin • 1930

Architects: C.H. Page & Brother

This building's official name is the Heman Marion Sweatt Travis County Courthouse, after the first Black student to be admitted to the UT law school. Not to diminish that historic achievement, but "Heman Sweatt" is a badass name in and of itself.

Navarro County Courthouse

21

Corsicana • 1905 • Restored 2016
Architect: J.E. Flanders

This courthouse is definitely striking, though a bit boxy, like your kid made it in Minecraft. Its 1880 predecessor, designed by Frederick Ernst Ruffini, was magnificent-looking—and yet they knocked it down after only 25 years, the jerks.

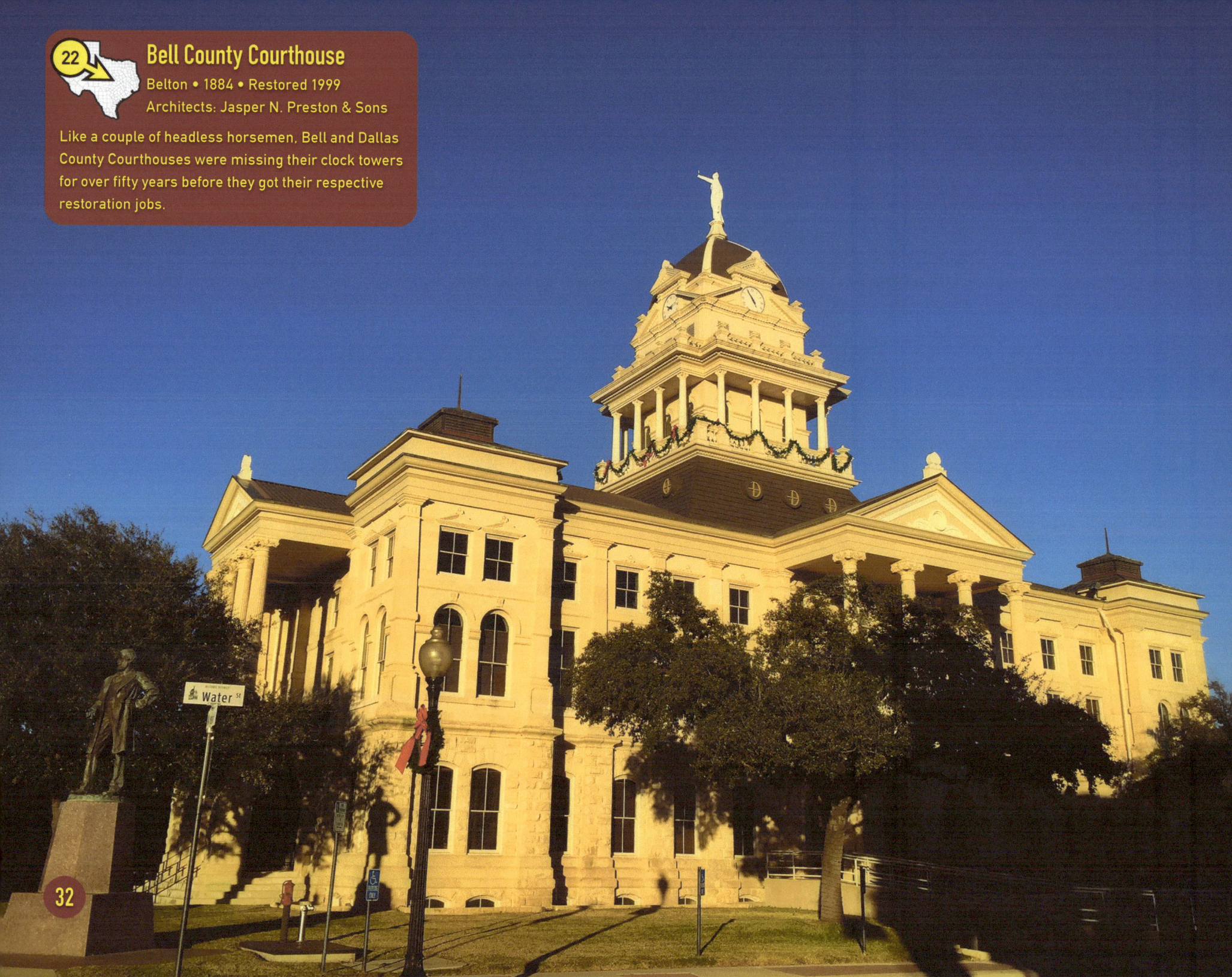

Bell County Courthouse

22

Belton • 1884 • Restored 1999
Architects: Jasper N. Preston & Sons

Like a couple of headless horsemen, Bell and Dallas
County Courthouses were missing their clock towers
for over fifty years before they got their respective
restoration jobs.

Water St

Dallas County Courthouse

23 →

Dallas • 1892 • Restored 2007
Architects: Orlopp & Kusener

The 1892 courthouse is fantastic, and even has a charming nickname: "Old Red." Peeking out from behind it is the 1966 courthouse, which would have a nickname like "Rectangle" if anyone ever cared enough to give it one.

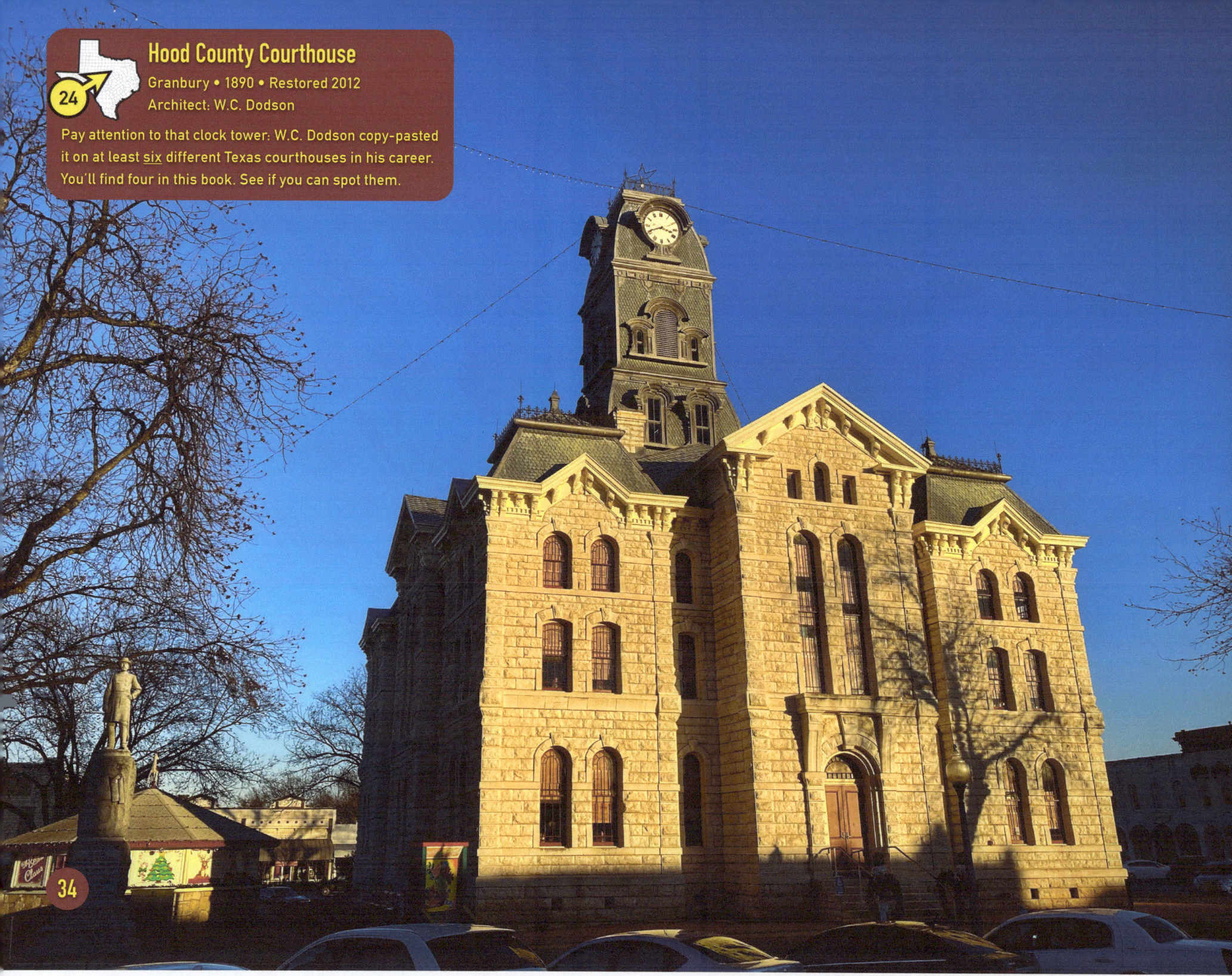

Hood County Courthouse

Granbury • 1890 • Restored 2012
Architect: W.C. Dodson

Pay attention to that clock tower: W.C. Dodson copy-pasted it on at least <u>six</u> different Texas courthouses in his career. You'll find four in this book. See if you can spot them.

Denton County Courthouse

Denton • 1896 • Restored 2004
Architect: W.C. Dodson

Many things make this Second Empire / Romanesque Revival building one of the loveliest courthouses in the state. My personal favorite detail is the li'l baby towers sprouting off of the main tower, like they're going to fly off and make courthouses of their own.

Tarrant County Courthouse

Fort Worth • 1895 • Restored 1983
Architects: Gunn & Curtis

26

A moment of silence for Birdville, which was the Tarrant County seat until an 1856 election moved it to Fort Worth WHILE THEY WERE BUILDING A COURTHOUSE. Today it's not even a city anymore. They did you wrong, Birdville.

Coryell County Courthouse

Gatesville • 1898
Architect: W.C. Dodson

According to the Texas State Historical Association, James Coryell was attacked and killed by Caddo Indians in 1837 while "raiding a bee tree." He probably would not have wanted us to know that little detail.

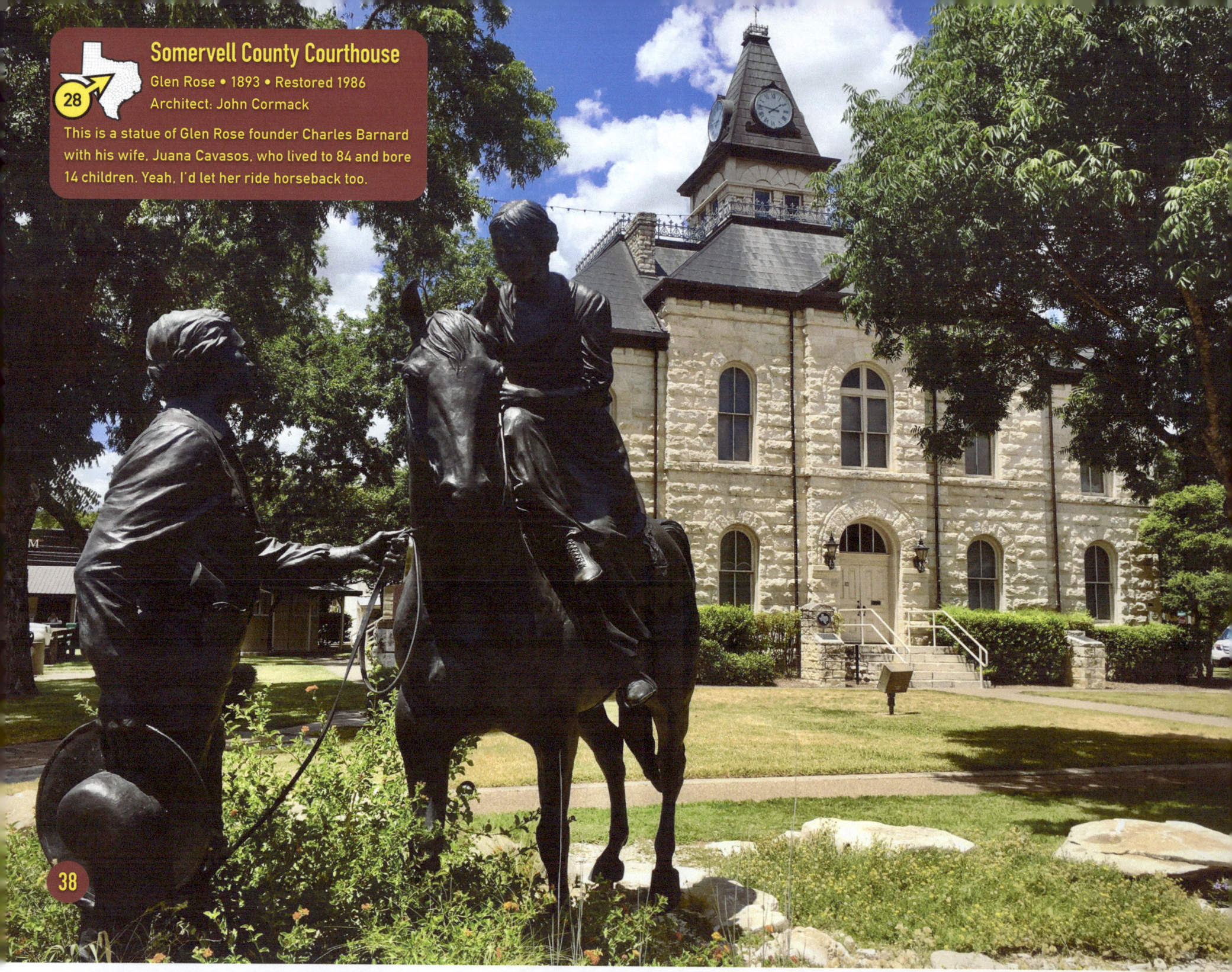

Somervell County Courthouse

Glen Rose • 1893 • Restored 1986
Architect: John Cormack

This is a statue of Glen Rose founder Charles Barnard with his wife, Juana Cavasos, who lived to 84 and bore 14 children. Yeah, I'd let her ride horseback too.

29

Williamson County Courthouse

Georgetown • 1911 • Restored 2007
Architect: Charles H. Page

You actually get a better view of the handsome copper dome driving up I-35 a mile away than you do from the courthouse square. I shoulda brought my drone. (I don't have a drone. Only nerds have drones. I am very cool.)

Wise County Courthouse

30

Decatur • 1897
Architect: J. Riely Gordon

You'll be seeing J. Riely Gordon's work a lot in this book, and these fraternal twins on opposite sides of DFW are two of his best.

Ellis County Courthouse
Waxahachie • 1897 • Restored 2003
Architect: J. Riely Gordon

A lucky fluke that I caught them both at golden hour.

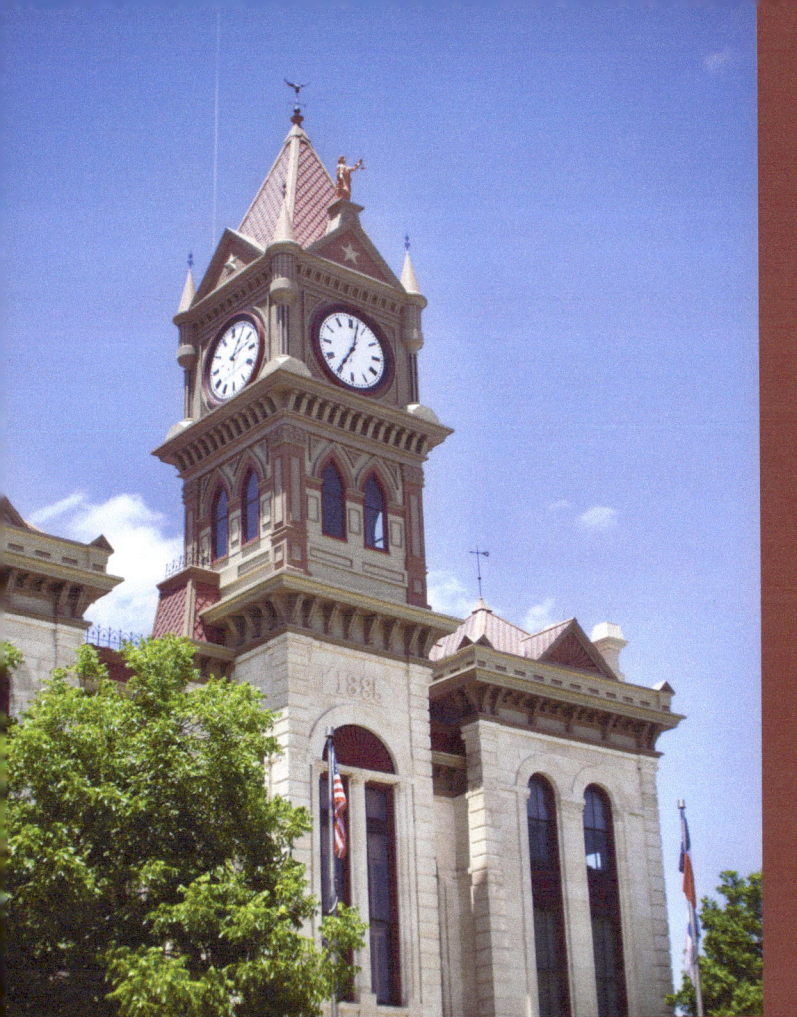

Bosque County Courthouse

Meridian • 1886 • Restored 2007
Architect: J.J. Kane

32

This gorgeous building got a bad nose job of a modernization way back in 1935. (Thanks a _lot_, WPA.) The towers and turrets made a glorious return in 2007.

Side note #1: It's BOS-kee. Not bos-KAY. Not bosk. Definitely not bos-KYOO-ee.

Side note #2: Meridian is nowhere near an actual meridian.

Rockwall County Courthouse

Rockwall • 2011

Architects: Brinkley Sargent Architects

Rockwall County tried to sneak this one by us. They erected a hulking building next to the I-30 access road, marooned in an ocean of empty parking spaces. Then they glued columns on the sides, bolted a dome on top, and figured we'd give it a pass.

Nice try, Rockwall County Courthouse. There are many kinds of ugly, and yours is the soulless kind.

UGLY!

ROCKWALL COUNTY COURTHOUSE

Erath County Courthouse

Stephenville • 1892 • Restored 2002
Architect: J. Riely Gordon

34

When this building was rehabilitated in 2002, the finial—that little doohickey on top of the tower—was removed for refurbishment. To the surprise of absolutely nobody, they found it pockmarked with bullet holes.

Hill County Courthouse

Hillsboro • 1890 • Rebuilt 1999
Architect: W.C. Dodson

35

This courthouse burned right to the ground on New Year's Day 1993, inspiring the Legislature to create the Texas Historic Courthouse Preservation Program that helped this and dozens of other courthouses to be restored and rebuilt. (The program needs a catchier name, but hey, so does this book.)

McLennan County Courthouse

Waco • 1902
Architect: J. Riely Gordon

Mr. Gordon went all-out on this one, from the dome patterned after St. Peter's to the squadron of protective eagles. In architectural jargon, I believe this is known as "extra."

36

Parker County Courthouse
Weatherford • 1886 • Restored 2005
Architects: Dodson & Dudley

37

The reported construction cost for this building was $55,555.55. I call shenanigans!

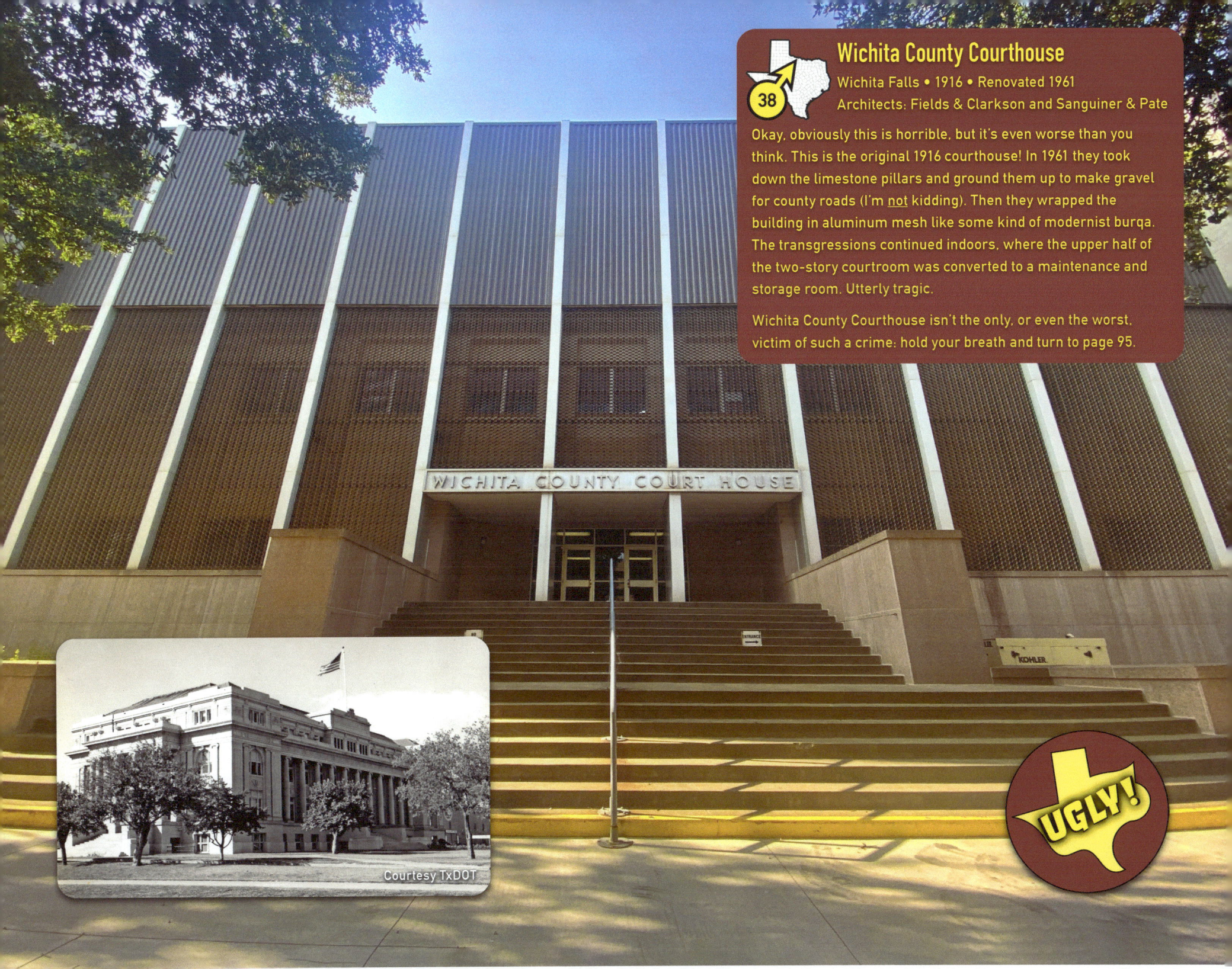

Wichita County Courthouse

Wichita Falls • 1916 • Renovated 1961
Architects: Fields & Clarkson and Sanguiner & Pate

Okay, obviously this is horrible, but it's even worse than you think. This is the original 1916 courthouse! In 1961 they took down the limestone pillars and ground them up to make gravel for county roads (I'm *not* kidding). Then they wrapped the building in aluminum mesh like some kind of modernist burqa. The transgressions continued indoors, where the upper half of the two-story courtroom was converted to a maintenance and storage room. Utterly tragic.

Wichita County Courthouse isn't the only, or even the worst, victim of such a crime: hold your breath and turn to page 95.

38

WICHITA COUNTY COURT HOUSE

Courtesy TxDOT

UGLY!

ALL THE BEST TACOS

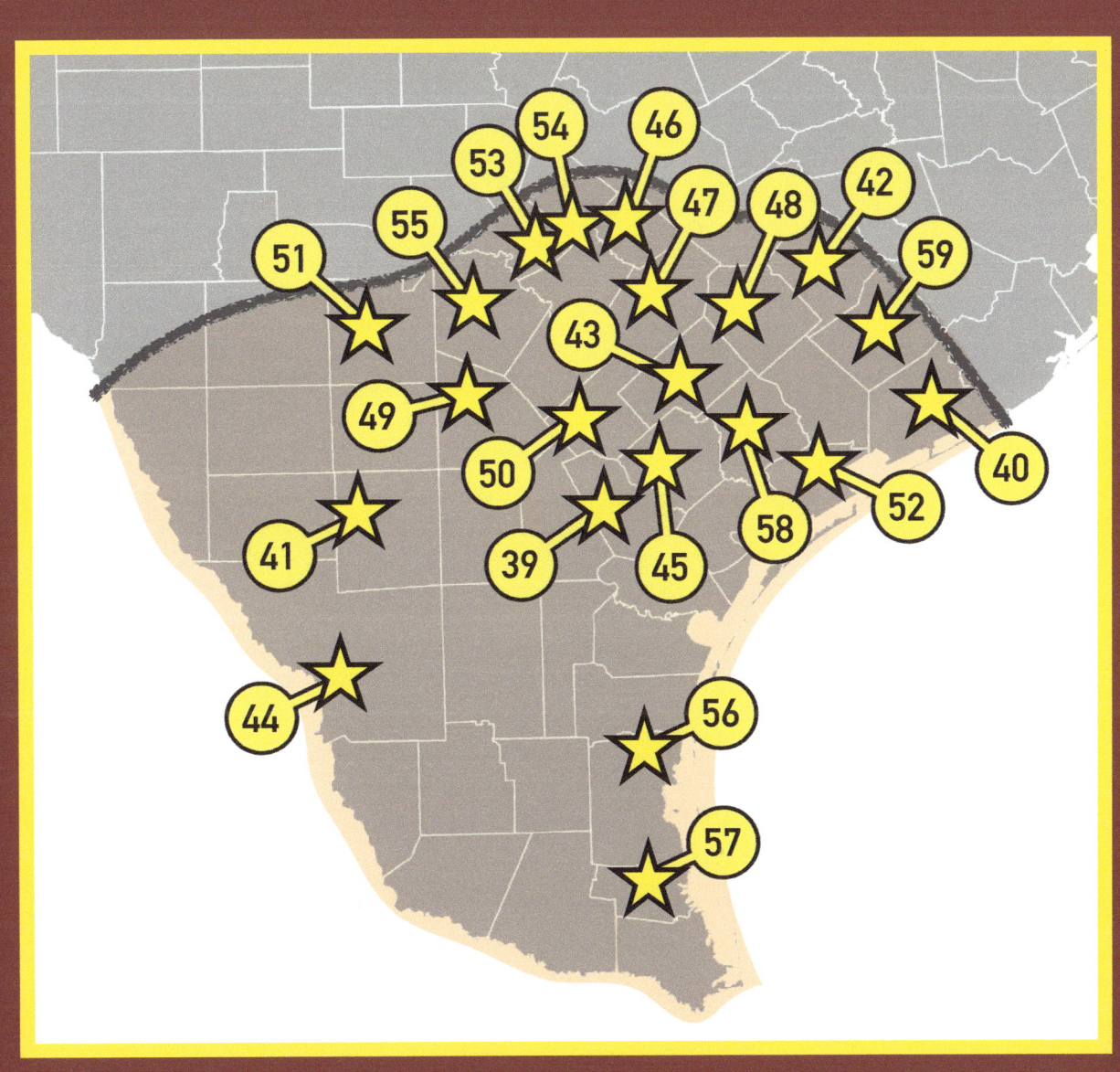

39

Bee County Courthouse
Beeville • 1912 • Restored 2006
Architects: Stephenson & Heldenfels

The courthouse is a bit hidden behind the trees,
but it's got a beehive-inspired dome and a Douglas
A-4 Skyhawk parked out front, and I couldn't bring
myself not to include it.

Eugene Heiner built a very nice courthouse for Matagorda County back in 1895, replaced by a handsome courthouse in 1928, and you would THINK I'd poop all over their concrete replacement from 1965—but ya know, I like it. It's got clean lines, and a handsome facade, and I'm gonna shut up before my lack of architectural training becomes too apparent.

MATAGORDA COUNTY COURT HOUSE

41 La Salle County Courthouse

Cotulla • 1931 • Restored 2013
Architect: Henry T. Phelps

Good example of how you can effectively bedazzle a boring courthouse building into something flashy. You've got your fancy door panels, your zigzag brickwork, and a golden eagle over the door. Sometimes less is more; sometimes more is more.

Colorado County Courthouse

42

Columbus • 1891 • Restored 2014
Architect: Eugene T. Heiner

Amusing story from the adjacent historical plaque:
"In 1909 a tornado severely damaged building. Large
bell in clock tower fell and was buried in the earth.
Job of clock-winder was subsequently canceled."

43

DeWitt County Courthouse

Cuero • 1897 • Restored 2007
Architects: A.O. Watson and Eugene Heiner

In the 1910s Cuero was home to the annual Cuero Turkey Trot,
where tens of thousands of turkeys were herded through town
to the delight of spectators. Today there's the Cuero Turkeyfest,
which according to its website is "home of Ruby Begonia—
fastest turkey in the South!"

Webb County Courthouse

Laredo • 1909
Architect: Alfred Giles

Alfred Giles worked on both sides of the border, with multiple civic buildings in northern Mexico in addition to his Texas work. The 1992 replacement for this courthouse, located on the adjacent block, is…fine.

Goliad County Courthouse

Goliad • 1894 • Restored 2003
Architect: Henri Guidon and/or Alfred Giles

There's some muddiness when deciding which architect—Alfred Giles or Henri Guidon—to credit for this courthouse and its sibling in Caldwell County. According to the Texas Historical Commission:

"[Courthouse] plans were sold to Caldwell County during [a] brief period when Guidon did not work with Giles; same plans subsequently sold to Goliad shortly after Guidon rejoined Giles practice; Giles later claimed both Caldwell and Goliad as his."

Sounds like there was some serious office drama going on.

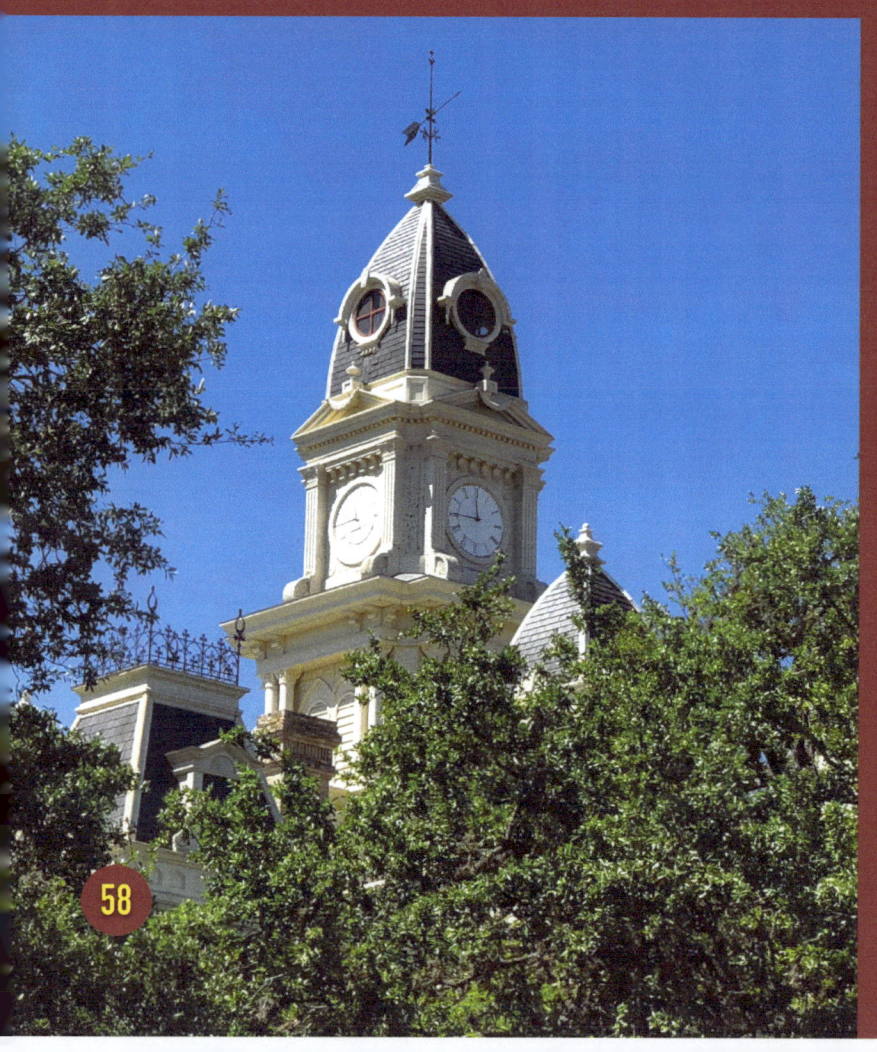

46 **Caldwell County Courthouse**
Lockhart • 1894 • Restored 2000
Architect: ¯_(ツ)_/¯

47

Gonzales County Courthouse

Gonzales • 1896 • Restored 1997
Architect: J. Riely Gordon

It's a pretty courthouse—I'm not suggesting otherwise—but I _am_ suggesting J. Riely Gordon was in an extremely "arches and columns" mood when he drew it up.

Lavaca County Courthouse

Hallettsville • 1897 • Restored 2010
Architect: Eugene T. Heiner

Even today there are fewer than 20,000 people in Lavaca County, so I'm not sure building a 170-foot-tall courthouse was strictly necessary. But I obviously appreciate the effort.

49 Atascosa County Courthouse

Jourdanton • 1912 • Restored 2003
Architect: Henry T. Phelps

Symmetry fans will bite their lips seductively at this courthouse, which sits within a circular drive and is almost identical on all four sides.

Karnes County Courthouse

50

Karnes City • 1894 • Restored 2018
Architect: John Cormack

The clock tower was removed in the 1920s and not restored until the 2010s, so this building has been towerless for the majority of its life. The rededication ceremony happened the week before I visited in 2018.

KARNES LAND TITLE CO., INC.

Medina County Courthouse

51

Hondo • 1892 • Renovated 1942
Architects: Martin, Byrnes, & Johnston

During World War II they demolished the clock tower and added the wings, but the result is _much_ better than these mid-century restorations tended to go. A recent proposal to restore the 1892 appearance was rejected, so this is what we get.

Courtesy TxDOT

CALHOUN COUNTY COURT HOUSE

53 **Comal County Courthouse**
New Braunfels • 1898 • Restored 2013
Architect: J. Riely Gordon

Another case of light self-plagiarism from J. Riely Gordon, who duplicated some architectural work when he built Lee County Courthouse (page 19) the next year.

I vote for more pink courtrooms.

Hays County Courthouse

54

San Marcos • 1908 • Restored 1998
Architects: C.H. Page & Brother

I don't want to make this book about me, but I do want to share the very next photo I took after this one. →

Bexar County Courthouse

San Antonio • 1892 • Restored 2015
Architect: J. Riely Gordon

Bexar County Courthouse is as quirky as it is beautiful. It was planted on the edge of the Main Plaza where San Antonio was first founded and grew southward over the years, away from the plaza, with various expansions creating a long and lumpy shape that gradually filled the block. In the '60s and '70s they added windowless cuboid extensions to the back side of the building, because OF COURSE THEY FREAKING DID.

But the front facade that faces the plaza—with its charmingly mismatched towers, rose windows, and terracotta frieze—remained intact and stunning. The 2015 restoration smartly excised the modernist tumors from the courthouse's butt while preserving the more tasteful 1920s additions. Today you can safely visit the building without muttering to yourself "What in the name of William Barrett Travis were they thinking?"

Kenedy County Courthouse

56

Sarita • 1917 • Restored 2010
Architect: Henry T. Phelps

Willacy County built its courthouse in Sarita, but in 1922, Kenedy County was established from portions of other counties—which, confusingly, included Sarita. That makes this the only building in Texas to have been courthouse for two different counties.

Willacy County Courthouse

Raymondville • 1922
Architect: Henry T. Phelps

This in turn meant Willacy County needed a second courthouse, and Henry Phelps didn't seem to mind doing the same job twice. (That tree in the foreground is a bit of a drama queen, ain't it?)

57

58

Victoria County Courthouse

Victoria • 1892 • Restored 2001
Architect: J. Riely Gordon

Just out of frame to the right is the mausoleum-inspired 1967 courthouse, connected to this one via covered walkway like a blood-sucking parasite.

Wharton County Courthouse

Wharton • 1889 • Restored 2007
Architect: Eugene T. Heiner

Someone explain to me why people still fly the Vietnam-era POW/MIA flag as though it's an ongoing national crisis.

I was kidding. Do NOT explain that to me. Turn off the Caps Lock key and step away from the Twitter app.

73

WINDMILLS & HABOOBS

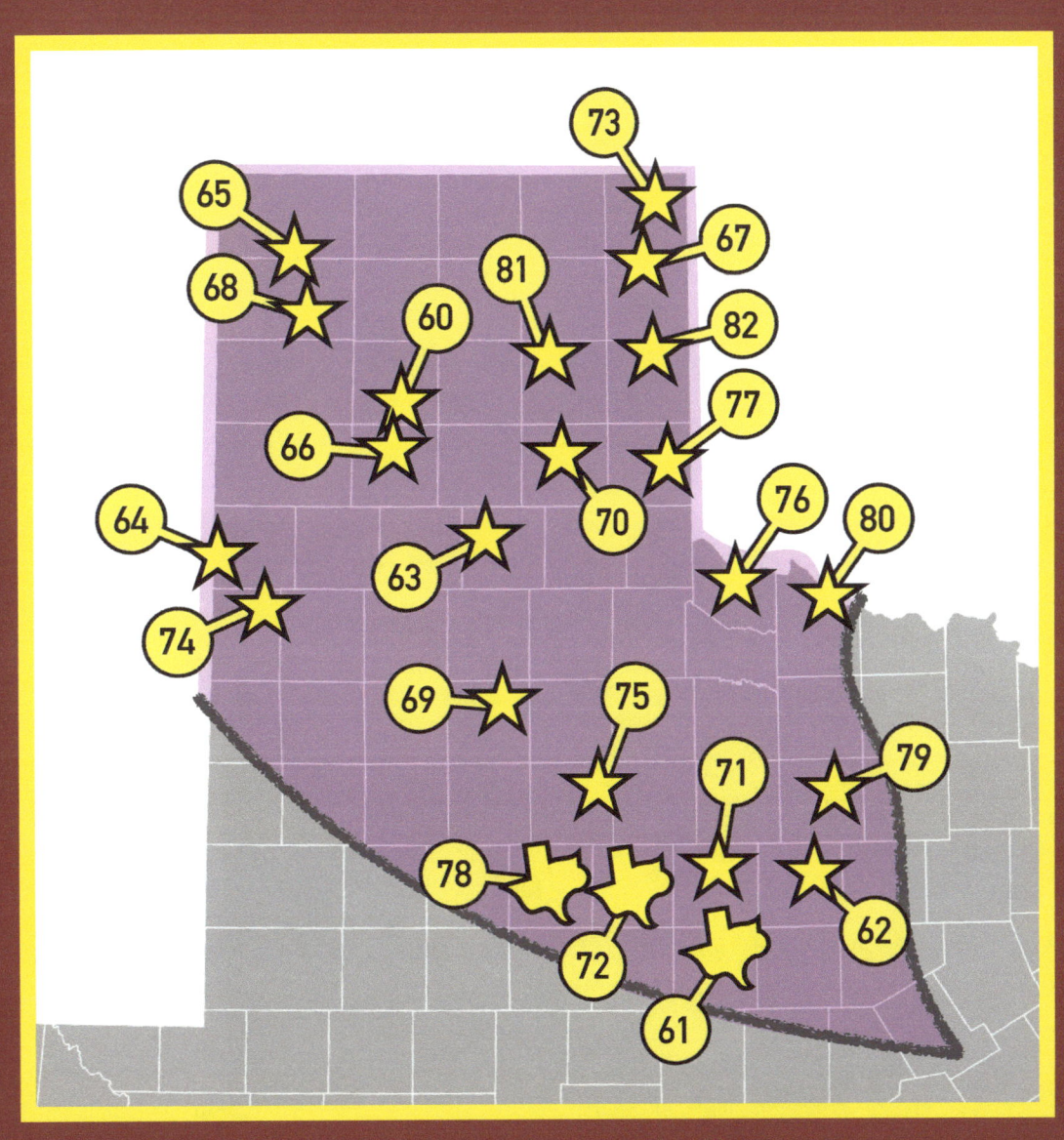

Potter County Courthouse

Amarillo • 1932 • Restored 2012
Architects: Townes, Lightfoot, & Funk

Hiding behind this imposing edifice you'll find the "new" Potter County Courthouse completed in 1986. Just look around for the concrete geometric edifice straight out of Robocop.

Fun trivia: one day in 1995, county officials mistakenly flew the Chilean flag over the courthouse.

Taylor County Courthouse

Abilene • 1972
Architects: Tittle, Luther, Loving, & Lee

I admit to discovering, long after my visit, that I'd actually photographed the <u>side</u> of the building. The front is hardly any different, though—go ahead, Google it.

The attractive 1914 courthouse stands right across the street, muttering something about kids these days.

61

TAYLOR COUNTY COURTHOUSE
300 OAK STREET

UGLY!

Shackelford County Courthouse

Albany • 1883 • Restored 2001
Architect: J.E. Flanders

This was the first courthouse to be restored under the Texas Historic Courthouse Preservation Program, which has since rehabilitated over 70 courthouses and counting. Shackelford County was a good candidate, since it's one of only two surviving courthouses out of nine designed by J.E. Flanders. (See page 31 for the other.)

62

78

Briscoe County Courthouse

Silverton • 1922
Architects: Smith & Townes

I have to admit I never saw "The Adventures of Brisco County, Junior," which is probably depriving me of a great joke right now. I have failed you all.

63

BRISCOE COUNTY 1922

Parmer County Courthouse

Farwell • 1916
Architect: C. Risser

Nuzzled up against the border with New Mexico is the third of the courthouse quadruplets (see page 15 for the first two). This one is the least like its siblings; the front doors are now permanently blocked off by an elevator.

64

Dallam County Courthouse
Dalhart • 1922
Architects: Smith & Townes

And nuzzled up against the border with Hartley County is the fourth of the siblings. (That toy soldier in the shadows is kinda menacing, if you ask me.)

Randall County Courthouse

Canyon • 1909 • Restored 2010
Architect: Robert G. Kirsch

In 2006 they made a new county courthouse out of an old Wal-Mart out on the highway. God, I wish I were joking.

82

Hemphill County Courthouse
Canadian • 1909
Architect: Robert G. Kirsch

Canadian is named for the nearby Canadian River, although nobody seems to know why the Canadian River is named that. I can personally vouch that it's way the hell north, though.

Hartley County Courthouse

Channing • 1906
Architect: O.G. Roquemore

In 1896 the county voted to move its seat from Hartley to Channing, whereupon a group of XIT Ranch cowboys put the old courthouse on wheels and rolled it 15 miles down the road. A decade later they said "never mind" and built this one instead. Sorry about that, cowboys.

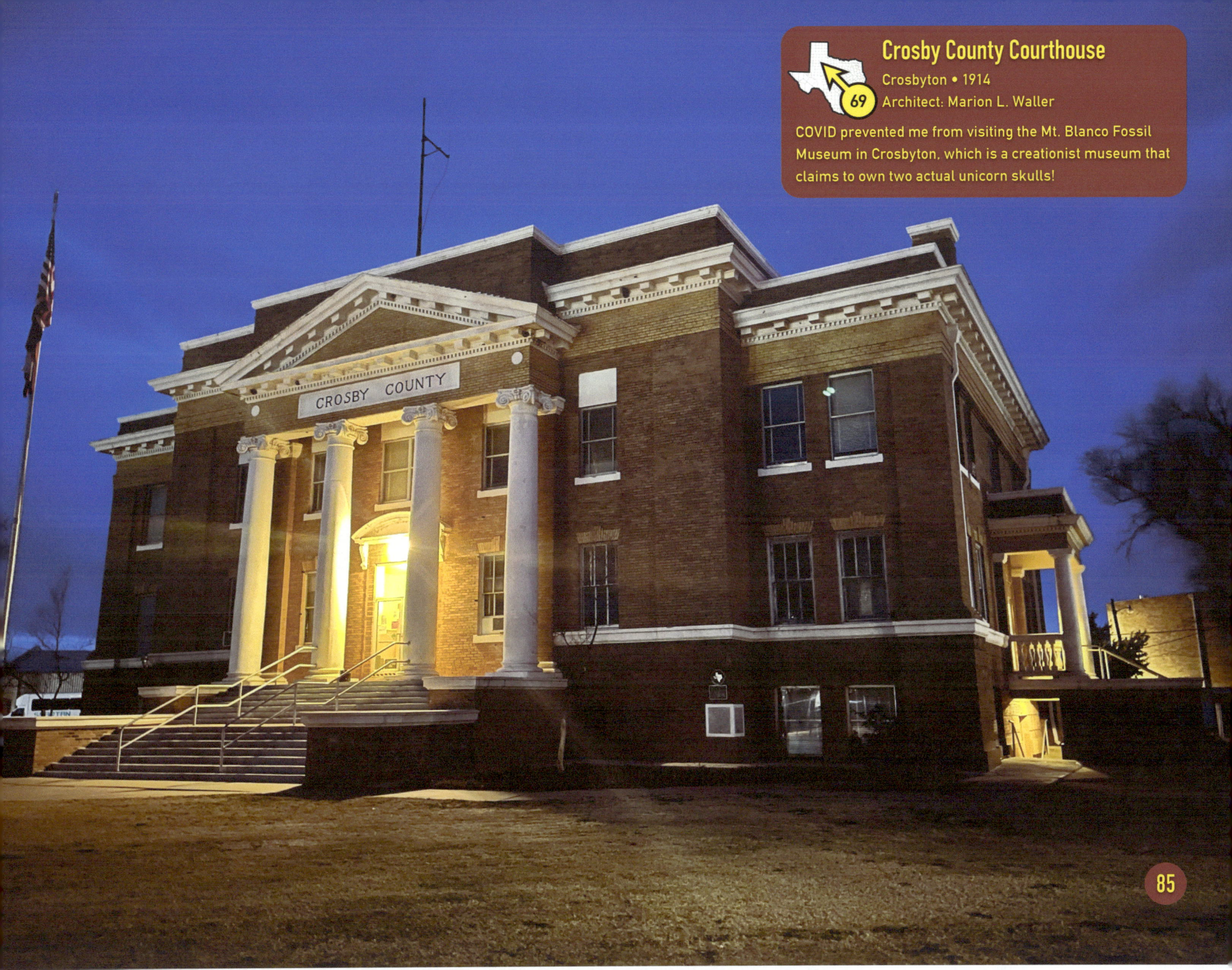

Crosby County Courthouse

Crosbyton • 1914
Architect: Marion L. Waller

69

COVID prevented me from visiting the Mt. Blanco Fossil Museum in Crosbyton, which is a creationist museum that claims to own two actual unicorn skulls!

CROSBY COUNTY

Donley County Courthouse

Clarendon • 1890 • Restored 2003
Architects: Charles Bulger & Isaac Rapp

In the 1930s, damage from a tornado forced the county to demolish everything above the second floor, and thus it remained until the big 2003 restoration. This might be the only completely asymmetrical courthouse in Texas, and it's all the prettier for it.

Jones County Courthouse

Anson • 1910

Architect: Elmer G. Withers

When they were first built, the Jones and Swisher County Courthouses were fraternal twins. As you'll see on page 127, the two buildings have aged rather differently.

71

UGLY!

Fisher County Courthouse

Roby • 1973

72 Architects: Lovett & Sellar & Associates

For another wild swing in courthouse quality, you can drive a mere 29 miles west from Anson, where Fisher County seems to have replaced its beautiful 1910 courthouse with my elementary school.

Courtesy courthousehistory.com

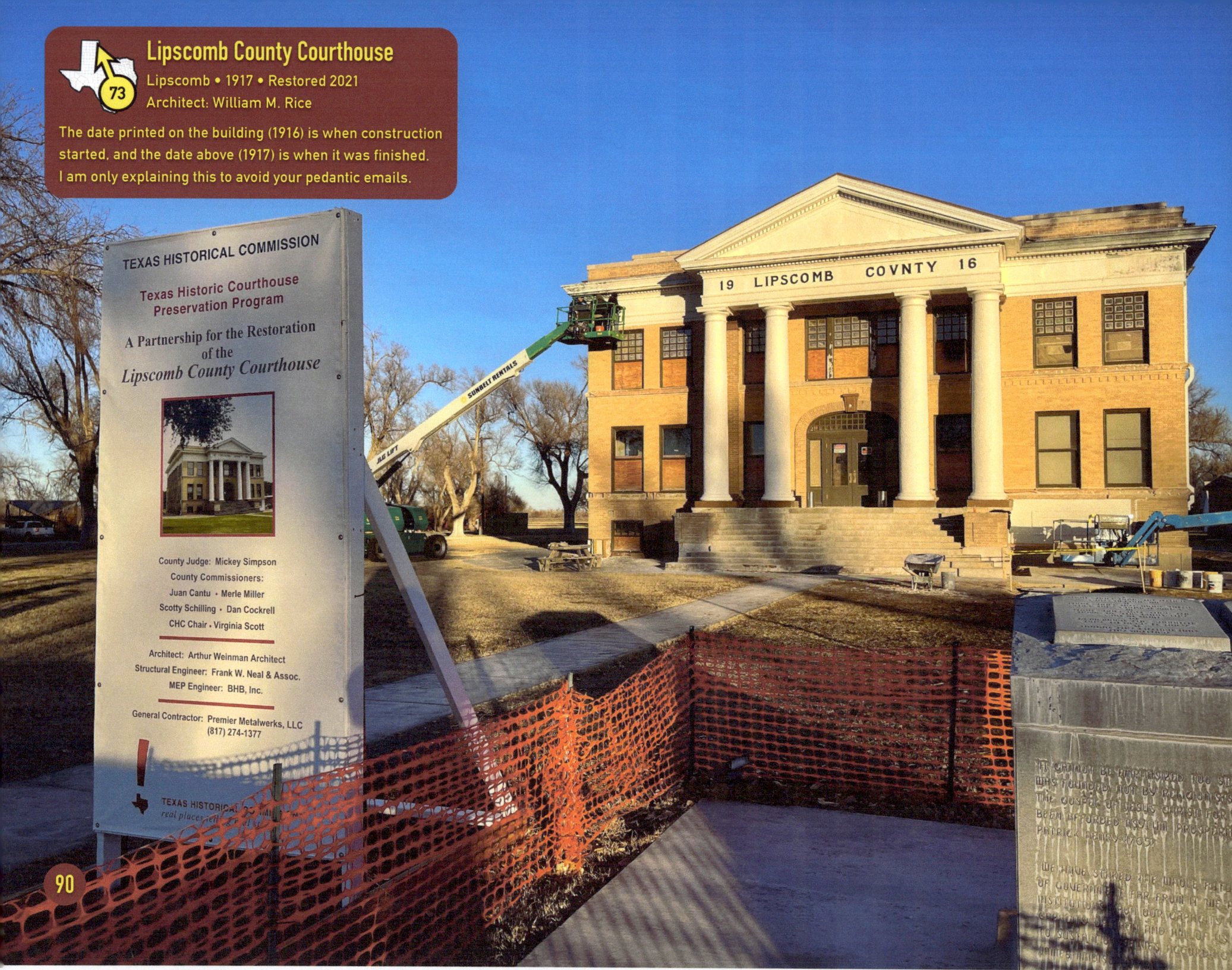

Lipscomb County Courthouse

73

Lipscomb • 1917 • Restored 2021
Architect: William M. Rice

The date printed on the building (1916) is when construction started, and the date above (1917) is when it was finished. I am only explaining this to avoid your pedantic emails.

TEXAS HISTORICAL COMMISSION

Texas Historic Courthouse
Preservation Program

A Partnership for the Restoration
of the
Lipscomb County Courthouse

County Judge: Mickey Simpson
County Commissioners:
Juan Cantu • Merle Miller
Scotty Schilling • Dan Cockrell
CHC Chair • Virginia Scott

Architect: Arthur Weinman Architect
Structural Engineer: Frank W. Neal & Assoc.
MEP Engineer: BHB, Inc.

General Contractor: Premier Metalwerks, LLC
(817) 274-1377

TEXAS HISTORICAL
real places tell

90

19 LIPSCOMB COVNTY 16

Bailey County Courthouse

Muleshoe • 1925
Architect: M.C. Butler

Muleshoe is home to the National Mule Memorial, which is apparently just a statue of a mule. I did not visit.

74

-19-BAILEY-COUNTY-COURT-HOUSE-25-

Kent County Courthouse

Jayton • 1957
75 Architect: Wyatt Hedrick

Look, sometimes I'm gonna think a boxy mid-century courthouse is pretty, and we're all just gonna be cool about it.

KENT COUNTY COURT HOUSE

Hardeman County Courthouse

Quanah • 1908 • Restored 2014
Architect: R.H. Stuckey

76

Quanah Parker and his mother, Cynthia Ann Parker, are two of the most fascinating characters in Texas history; you should really put this book down and go read about them instead. Quanah himself was in attendance when the town named for him was founded in 1884—how often has that ever happened?

Collingsworth County Courthouse

Wellington • 1931
Architects: Berry & Hatch

Wellington was voted the county seat in 1891 when its backers offered free town lots to those who voted for it. The golden age of voter fraud.

77

Scurry County Courthouse

Snyder • 1911 • Entombed 1972
Architects: Lang & Witchell / Joseph D. Hinton

In a word, it's terrifying: a windowless tomb, brutalism at its most brutal, a shoo-in for the "ten ugliest" list. But the moment of abject horror arrives when you realize that they didn't simply raze the lovely former courthouse, like so many other Texas counties have done. This is the original building, sealed behind granite panels, its screams unheard by passing citizens for fifty years now. Edgar Allan Poe would blush.

You can see this building's original form over in Gainesville where its twin, Cooke County Courthouse, has been lovingly restored.

UGLY!

Scurry County Court House,
Snyder, Texas.

Courtesy courthousehistory.com

SCURRY COUNTY COURTHOUSE

95

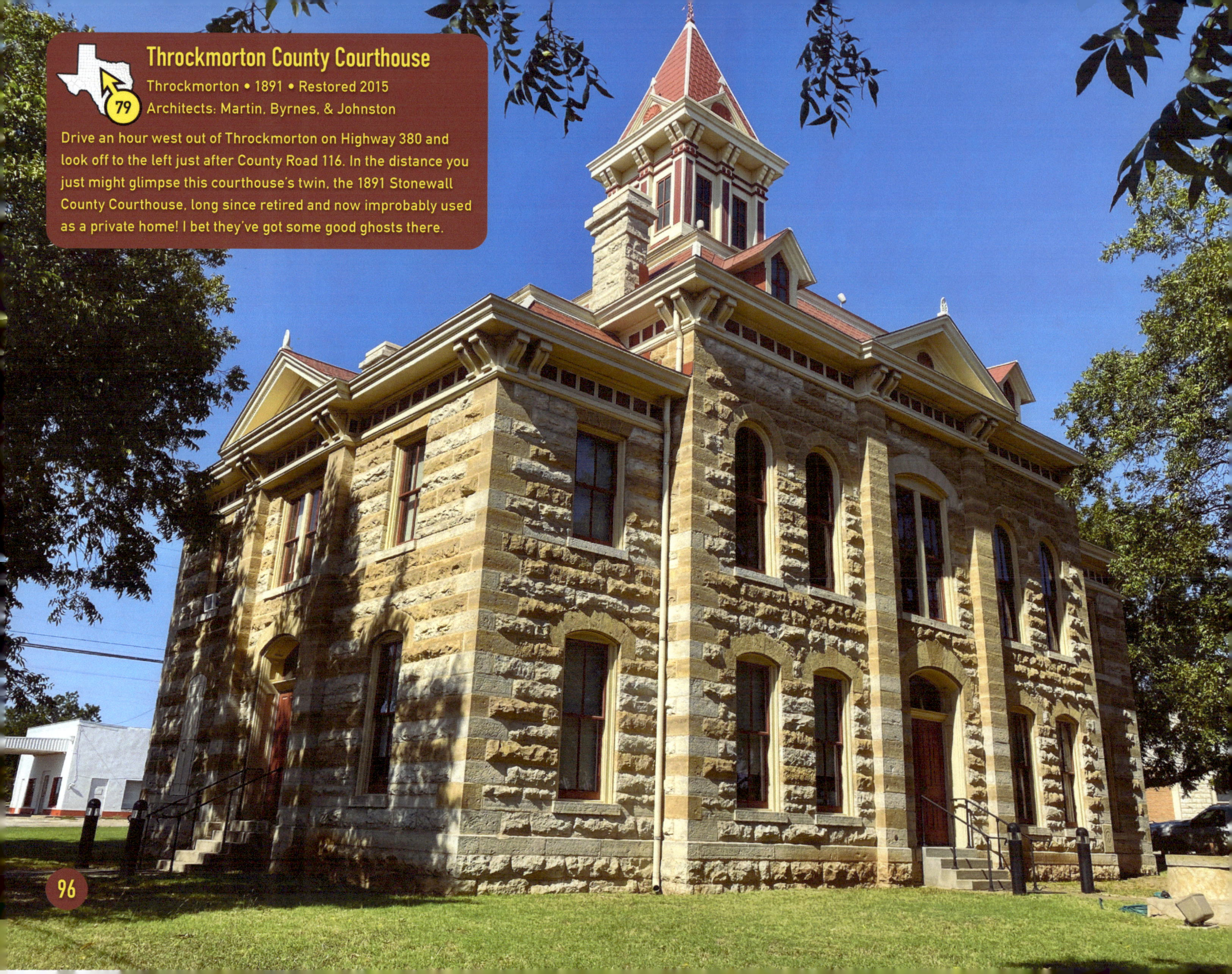

79

Throckmorton County Courthouse

Throckmorton • 1891 • Restored 2015
Architects: Martin, Byrnes, & Johnston

Drive an hour west out of Throckmorton on Highway 380 and look off to the left just after County Road 116. In the distance you just might glimpse this courthouse's twin, the 1891 Stonewall County Courthouse, long since retired and now improbably used as a private home! I bet they've got some good ghosts there.

Wilbarger County Courthouse

Vernon • 1928
Architects: Voelcker & Dixon

Josiah Wilbarger lived nowhere near here, and his big claim to fame was being scalped by Comanche Indians and surviving the ordeal, so the barrier for having a Texas county named after you seems...low.

GRAY COVNTY COVRT HOVSE

Gray County Courthouse

Pampa • 1928 • Restored 2003
Architect: W.R. Kaufman

Gray County built itself a shiny new oil-money courthouse in 1928, just in time for Black Tuesday (the 1929 stock crash) and Black Sunday (the 1935 dust storm). Still standing though!

81

Wheeler County Courthouse

Wheeler • 1925 • Restored 2004
Architect: E.H. Eads

20 minutes northwest of Wheeler you can find the middle-of-nowhere crossroads where Tom Hanks stood in the film "Cast Away." It is an accurate depiction of this part of Texas.

WHEELER · COUNTY · COURT · HOUSE

99

"ARE WE THERE YET?"

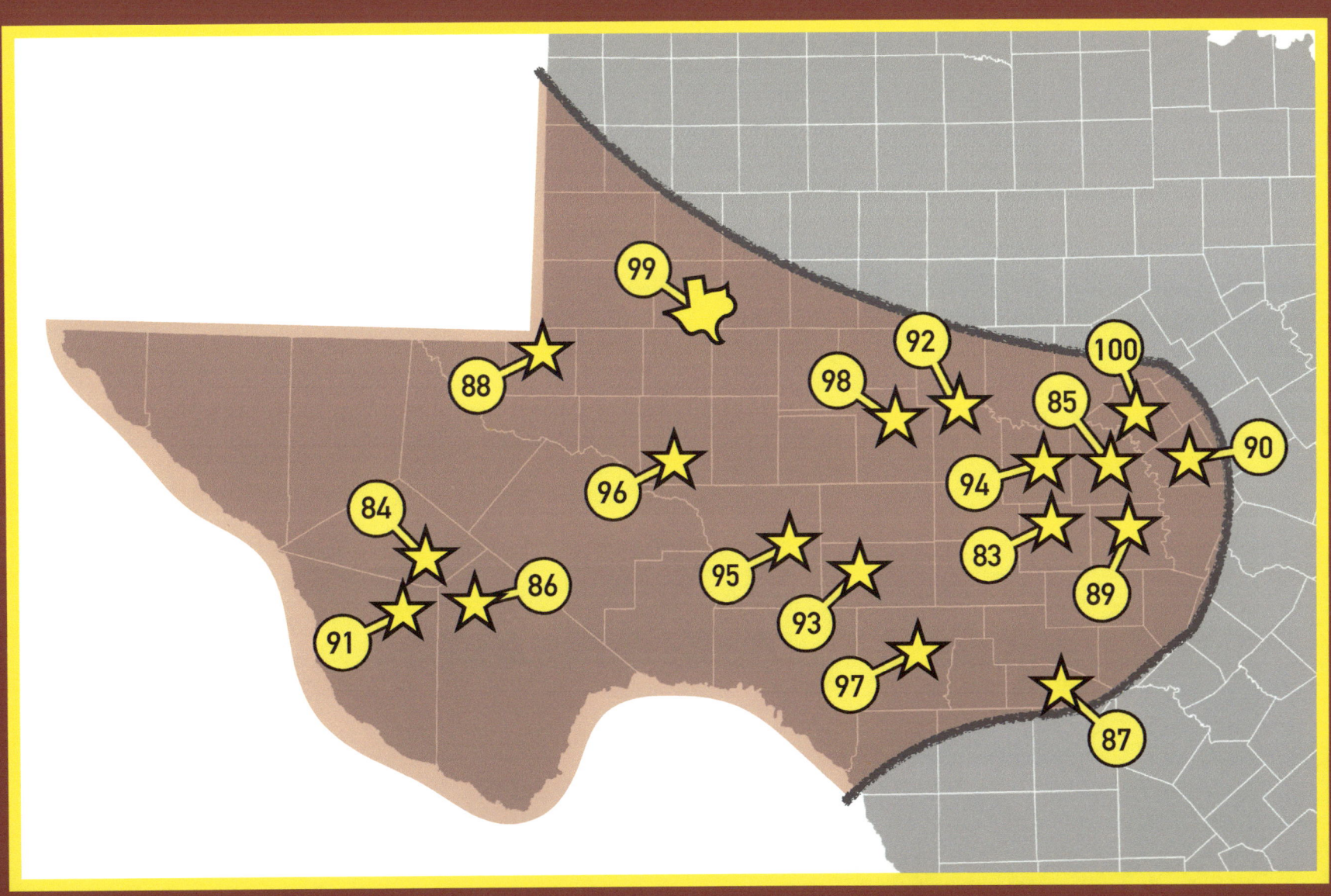

83 Mason County Courthouse

Mason • 1909 • Destroyed 2021
Architects: E.C. Hosford & Co.

An arsonist burned Mason County Courthouse to the ground in 2021, just as I was starting to design this book. It was rededicated in 2023.

...Yes, it took them less time to rebuild a whole damn courthouse than it took me to make a courthouse book.

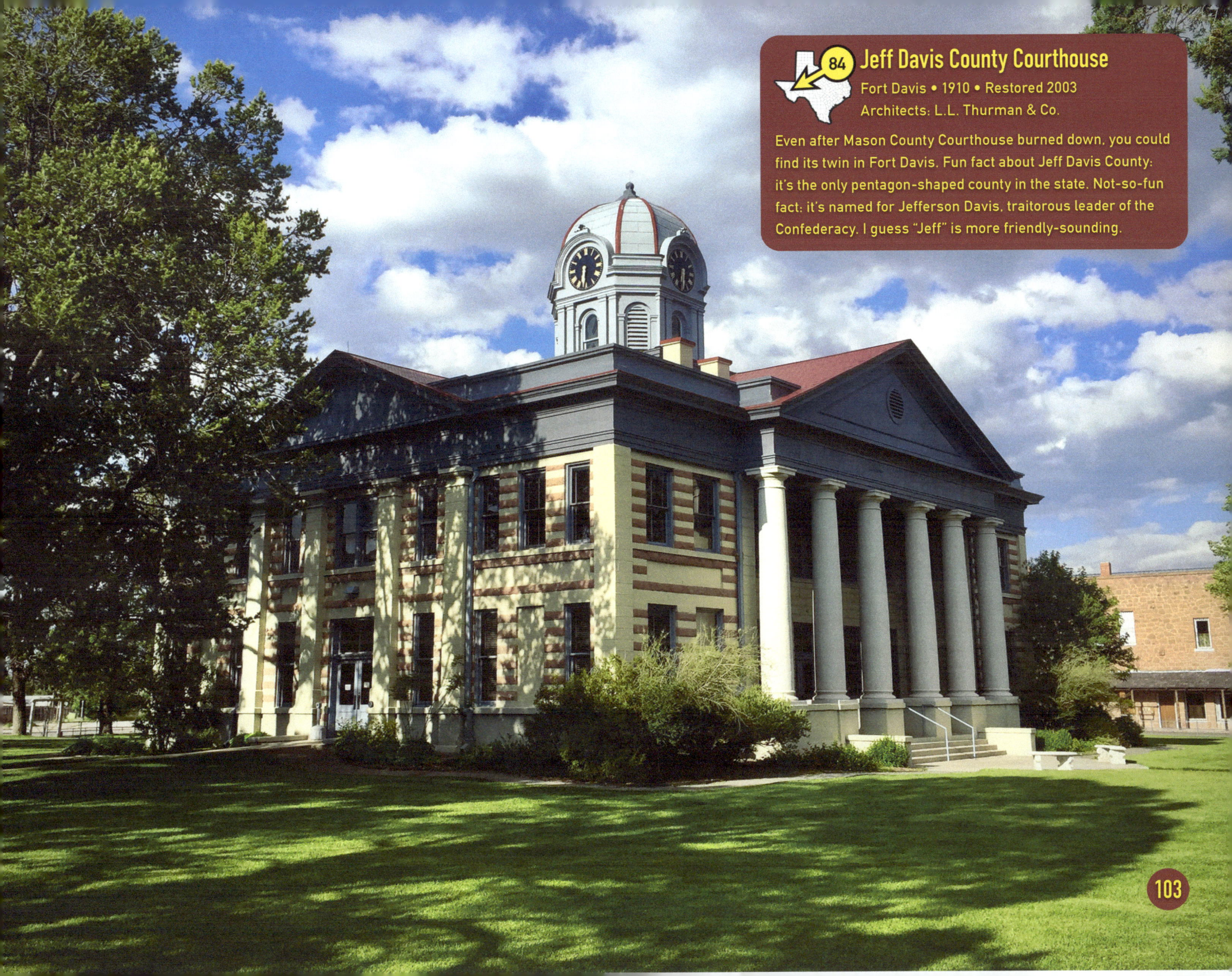

84 Jeff Davis County Courthouse

Fort Davis • 1910 • Restored 2003
Architects: L.L. Thurman & Co.

Even after Mason County Courthouse burned down, you could find its twin in Fort Davis. Fun fact about Jeff Davis County: it's the only pentagon-shaped county in the state. Not-so-fun fact: it's named for Jefferson Davis, traitorous leader of the Confederacy. I guess "Jeff" is more friendly-sounding.

85 San Saba County Courthouse

San Saba • 1911 • Restored 2020
Architects: Chamberlin & Co.

San Saba was utterly lawless at the end of the 19th century, to the point that anti-mob militias became mobs themselves and the Texas Rangers instituted martial law in 1896. So the motto over the courthouse entrance has an aspirational vibe.

SAN SABA

FROM THE PEOPLE TO THE PEOPLE

86 Brewster County Courthouse

Alpine • 1887
Architect: Thomas Lovell

The front of the courthouse is hidden by trees, but the back is handsome too. For your next Texas trivia contest: Brewster County is bigger than Connecticut, but has fewer residents than Bastrop.

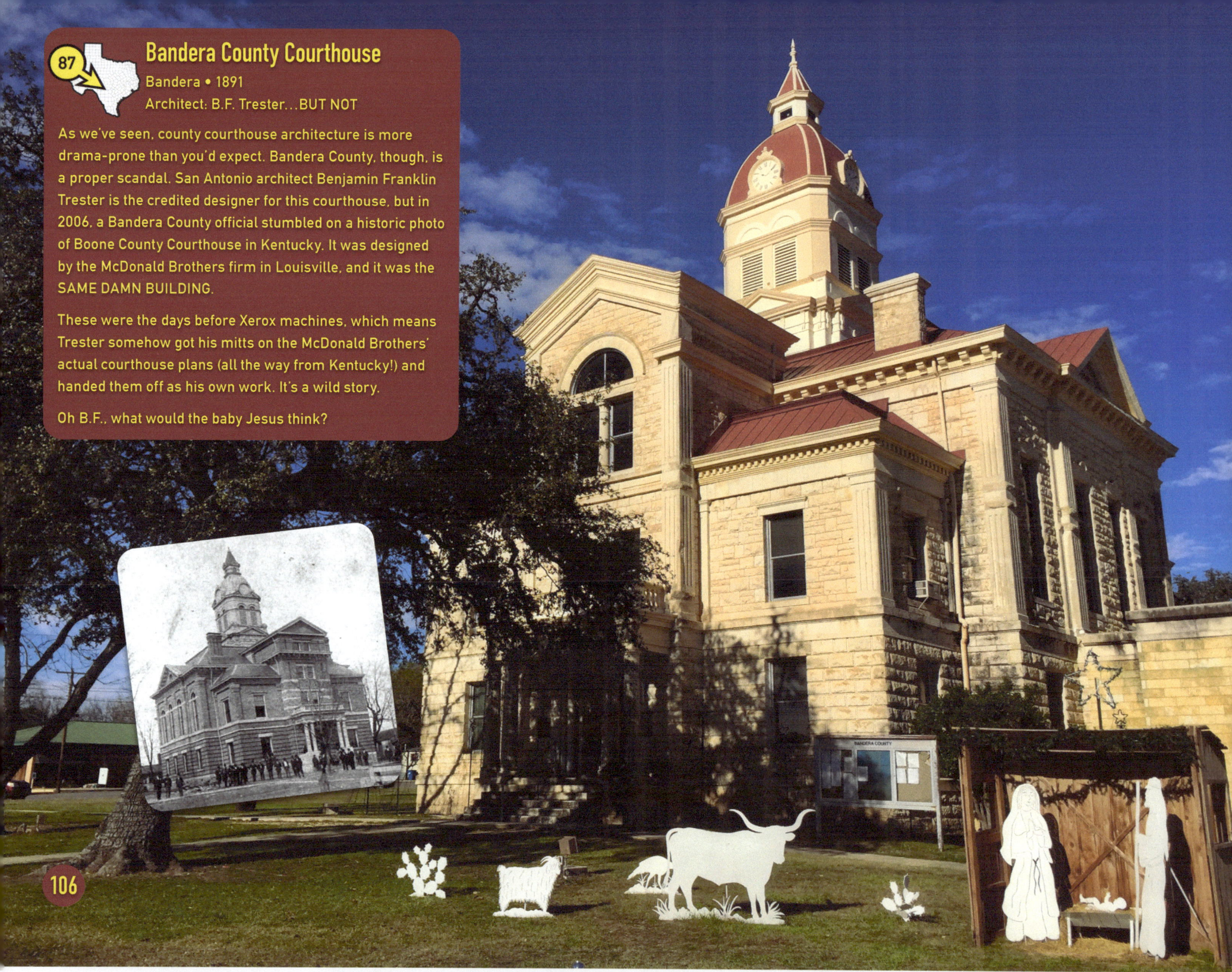

Bandera County Courthouse

Bandera • 1891
Architect: B.F. Trester...BUT NOT

As we've seen, county courthouse architecture is more drama-prone than you'd expect. Bandera County, though, is a proper scandal. San Antonio architect Benjamin Franklin Trester is the credited designer for this courthouse, but in 2006, a Bandera County official stumbled on a historic photo of Boone County Courthouse in Kentucky. It was designed by the McDonald Brothers firm in Louisville, and it was the SAME DAMN BUILDING.

These were the days before Xerox machines, which means Trester somehow got his mitts on the McDonald Brothers' actual courthouse plans (all the way from Kentucky!) and handed them off as his own work. It's a wild story.

Oh B.F., what would the baby Jesus think?

88

Winkler County Courthouse

Kermit • 1929
Architect: David S. Castle

Is it a pretty courthouse? Yes. Is it the absolute prettiest courthouse in Texas? No. Was I influenced in my choice because the name of the town is Kermit? Maybe.

Llano County Courthouse
Llano • 1893 • Restored 2002
Architects: A.O. Watson & Jacob Larmour

According to texasescapes.com, "The architectural firm of Larmour & Watson was apparently dissolved during the construction of this building, which is why only Watson's name is on the cornerstone." Man, are Texas county courthouse architects a teen soap opera or what?

If you're looking for affordable Austin real estate in the 21st century, Lampasas is a great place to start.

91

Presidio County Courthouse

Marfa • 1887 • Renovated 2002
Architect: Alfred Giles

I don't really have any snark here. Presidio County Courthouse is just lovely. Don't spend so much time looking for ghost lights or hippie artwork on your next road trip here that you miss paying a visit.

92

Concho County Courthouse

Paint Rock • 1886

Architects: Frederick & Oscar Ruffini

You can find near-identical-twin courthouses less than a hundred miles from each other in Paint Rock and Sonora. This was a popular design for the Ruffini brothers: there's a triplet still standing in Blanco, and two more copies once stood in Baird and Goldthwaite.

93 Sutton County Courthouse
Sonora • 1891 • Restored 2002
Architect: Oscar Ruffini

Frederick died in 1886, so Oscar got sole credit for this one.

McCulloch County Courthouse

Brady • 1899 • Restored 2009
Architects: Martin & Moodie

Marty McFly would be shocked at the number of courthouse clock towers that need saving in this state.

Crockett County Courthouse

Ozona • 1902
Architect: Oscar Ruffini

Can't they, like, paint one on there?

96 Upton County Courthouse

Rankin • 1926 • Renovated 1958
Architects: David S. Castle / Leonard F. Crockett

See? I'm not opposed to ALL modernist renovations. In the '50s Upton County gave its pedestrian bread box of a courthouse an extreme makeover that turned out quite interesting. I'm sure Upton County's 3,300 residents appreciate it.

Courtesy TxDOT

The former county seat, Upland, was one of many Texas towns that were bypassed by the railroad when it was built and subsequently abandoned. The former Upton County Courthouse is all that remains of the town, forgotten and crumbling on private land. It's spooky as heck, and as you'll see, it's not the only "life after people" courthouse in Texas.

117

Edwards County Courthouse

Rocksprings • 1891 • Restored 2014
Architects: Ben Davey & Bruno Schott

This poor girl burned in a fire in 1898 and was hit by a tornado in 1927. Even worse: a drop ceiling was installed in the 1960s! (Don't worry, they fixed it.)

When the state legislature formed Tom Green County in 1874, it was over 60,000 square miles—that's bigger than Georgia! The Lege later established 66 other counties from the land, but there's one weird vestigial reminder of this turkey carving: Tom Green is the only county with a panhandle.

Martin County Courthouse

Stanton • 1975

Architects: Riherd & Huckabee

Yet another lowest-bid courthouse that uses bits and bobs from its predecessor in a half-assed attempt at decoration—in this case a charmless gazebo that doesn't even keep the rain out.

Do I feel guilty about obscuring my picture of the courthouse itself with all these images and text blocks? Reader, I do not.

Courtesy TxDOT

Courtesy TxDOT

And no, I didn't forget about you, Waller County.

MARTIN COUNTY

UGLY!

Mills County Courthouse

Goldthwaite • 1913 • Restored 2011
Architect: Henry T. Phelps

In December 2020 I took a meandering four-day road trip around the Panhandle to visit the last three dozen courthouses on my checklist. Long after dark on the fourth day, I was almost back to Austin when I passed through Goldthwaite and saw Mills County Courthouse glowing brilliantly on the side of the road. I knew I already had a picture of this one, but naturally I stopped anyway.

This turned out to be the last courthouse picture I took before I moved away from Texas. Later on, I realized that my earlier picture (below) was from way back in 2014, long before this project was even a project. This makes Mills County, of all places, an unexpected bookend to this crazy undertaking.

Oh and the 1888 jail building next door is nice, but if you want a "Prettiest County Jailhouses in Texas" book, then you'll have to look elsewhere.

PARTICIPATION RIBBONS

It's hard to pick just 90 beautiful courthouses from so many options.
It's equally hard to pick just ten ugly ones. Here are a few of my favorite also-rans.

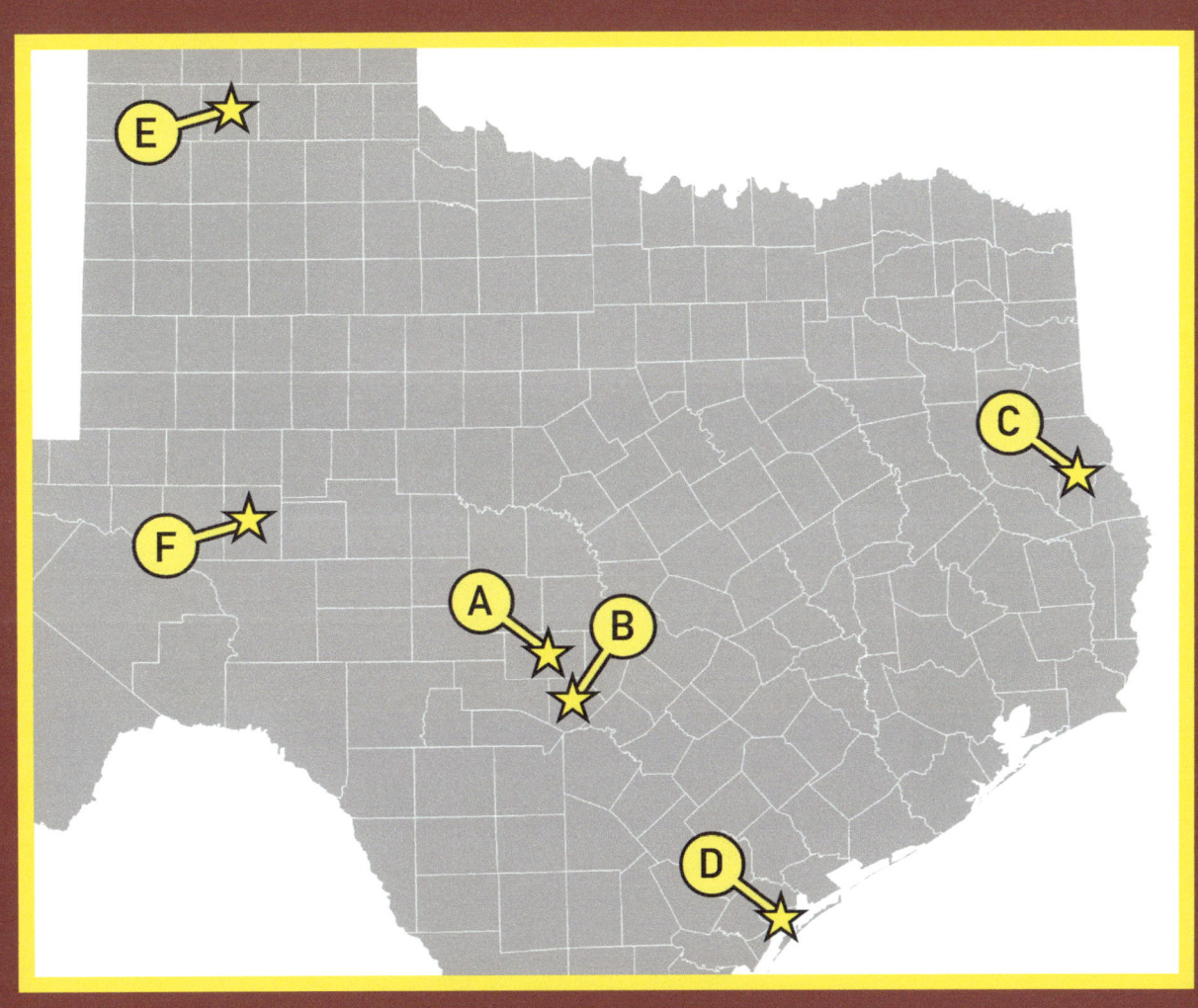

A

Gillespie County Courthouse

Fredericksburg • 1939

Architect: Edward Stein

You'd be mad if I made a whole courthouse book and didn't include this picture.

Kendall County Courthouse

Boerne • 1870 • Restored 2010
Architects: Philip Zoeller & J. F. Stendebach

An incredibly boring courthouse replaced the historic one in Boerne in 1998. I do need to show off the old courtroom, though. If "D" Magazine shared this picture in their next issue, every Highland Park housewife would be repainting their wooden floors with a diagonal checkerboard by year's end.

San Augustine County Courthouse

San Augustine • 1927 • Restored 2010
Architect: Shirley Simons

The 2011 Richard Linklater film "Bernie" fictionalizes a real-life trial in the San Augustine County courtroom, and weirdly, the movie courtroom is less attractive than the real thing.

Courtesy TxDOT

Aransas County Courthouse

Rockport • 1956 • Demolished 2018
Architect: Lynn A. Evans

The stunning 1889 Aransas County Courthouse was designed by hitmaker J. Riely Gordon and razed during the wrecking-ball-swingin' 1960s after they replaced it with a painfully dull affair. In 2017, Hurricane Harvey issued some karmic revenge.

True story: I drove around downtown Rockport for half an hour trying to find the damn courthouse before I realized that this concrete pad was it. A rather nice-looking replacement is due to be completed in 2023.

Courtesy courthousehistory.com

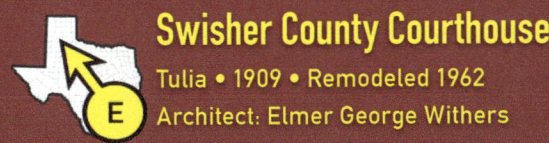

Swisher County Courthouse
Tulia • 1909 • Remodeled 1962
Architect: Elmer George Withers

Courtesy courthousehistory.com

Swisher County Courthouse was technically built in 1909, but the restoration following a 1962 fire was so thoroughly soul-draining that it'd be disingenuous to call it the "same building." (Flip back to Jones County Courthouse on page 88 to see what it could've been.) It's also seen more than its share of judicial ugliness, as author Nate Blakeslee documented in his 1999 book "Tulia: Race, Cocaine, and Corruption in a Small Texas Town."

In short, when I first saw this thing in 2014—a box of depression surrounded by a sea of pavement—it was easily on the Ten Ugliest list. Nate Blakeslee himself called it the "world's ugliest courthouse." But I happened to pass it again in 2020 and saw that it had received some landscaping and a minor facelift, which was just barely enough to keep it off my list of shame. (For now. You're on the bubble, Swisher County.)

127

Reagan County was established in 1903, and in 1911 voters built the county seat of Stiles at its center, featuring a fine limestone courthouse. But when the railroad came through a few years later, it missed Stiles by twenty miles. In short order the town was abandoned, and vanished without a trace—except for the courthouse, which now stands watch in an empty valley, exactly halfway between nothing and nowhere.

It's not as ancient as it looks—the building was used for various purposes until it fell victim to arson on Christmas Eve 1999. But when you spot it standing alone on the landscape as you come around the bend on State Highway 137, you'd be forgiven for thinking you'd discovered a thousand-year-old ruin. It is, strangely enough, my favorite courthouse I ever visited.

Reagan County Courthouse
Stiles • 1911 • Abandoned 1925

For the record, the modern Reagan County Courthouse—down the road in Big Lake, built in 1927—is perfectly respectable.

129

PICTURES FROM THE ROAD

I'm gonna be honest: Texas is mostly flat emptiness punctuated by gas stations and dollar stores. But when you hunt courthouses across the length and breadth of this enormous state, you inevitably encounter some beautiful sights. Here are just a few—brought to you by Dr Pepper, beef jerky, and the open road.

Clockwise from top left: Lockhart, Marfa, Leakey
Previous page: Edwards County

Clockwise from top left: Trinity, Hemphill County, Yoakum

Clockwise from top left: Stratford, Rocksprings, Fort Lancaster

Clockwise from top left: Merkel, Big Bend, Pearsall

135

THANKS AND CREDITS

Thanks first and foremost to the Texas Historic Courthouse Preservation Program (THCPP), which has been restoring and preserving Texas courthouses since 1999. Thanks also to the Texas Historical Commission (THC) and Texas State Historical Association (TSHA), and to the following:

- Kiki Hohnen, for the constant encouragement and support

- David Lampe, for helping me think of this dumb idea in the first place

- Chuy Zarate, for reminding me (frequently!) that courthouses are more than just buildings

- Ryan Schmidt, for a wide variety of help and advice

- My volunteer reviewers, whose feedback improved this book by orders of magnitude

- Jennie Fisher, who brought my book design to life

And some fellow courthouse aficionados:

- The contributors at texasescapes.com—particularly courthouse devotee Terry Jeanson—for being my first, best, utterly indispensable resource when researching courthouses

- The equally dedicated nerds at 254texascourthouses.net and texascourthouses.com

- Keith Vincent at courthousehistory.com for providing a few vintage postcard images I could find nowhere else

- Barclay Gibson for the tips on a couple of out-of-the-way former courthouses

Polk County Courthouse, Livingston

All present-day photos were taken by me between 2010 and 2020 using iPhones 4 through 12 (and in a few cases, my Canon T1i).

Most historic photos are from the 1939 photographic survey of Texas county courthouses by the Texas Department of Transportation (TxDOT). Others are as listed below:

- Page 13, 23, 89, 95, 126, 127: courthousehistory.com
- Page 31: Texas Historical Commission
- Page 106: Boone County Historic Preservation Review Board, via texasescapes.com

As I said at the beginning, there are already a lot of entries in the Texas-county-courthouse section of your local library. Here are a few of my direct competitors, but there could be more!

- June R. Welch & J. Larry Nance, "The Texas Courthouse" (1971 & 1984)
- Mavis P. Kelsey Sr. & Donald H. Dyal, "The Courthouses of Texas" (1993 & 2007)
- Curt Roberts, "A Photographic Tour of Texas County Courthouses" (2011)
- Brantley Hightower, "The Courthouses of Central Texas" (2015)

In addition to the one on page 34, you can find W.C. Dodson's distinctive courthouse tower on pages 46, 48, and 109.

Visit bit.ly/BanderaCourthouse for the full story on the (possibly) stolen plans for Bandera County Courthouse.

Construction and restoration dates differ in various sources, so suffice it to say: all dates given are approximate. I did my best.

Keep in touch at courthousebook.com, or check out my other Texas-themed endeavor: @UglyTexases on Instagram and other socials.

Limestone County Courthouse, Groesbeck

Floyd County Courthouse, Floydada

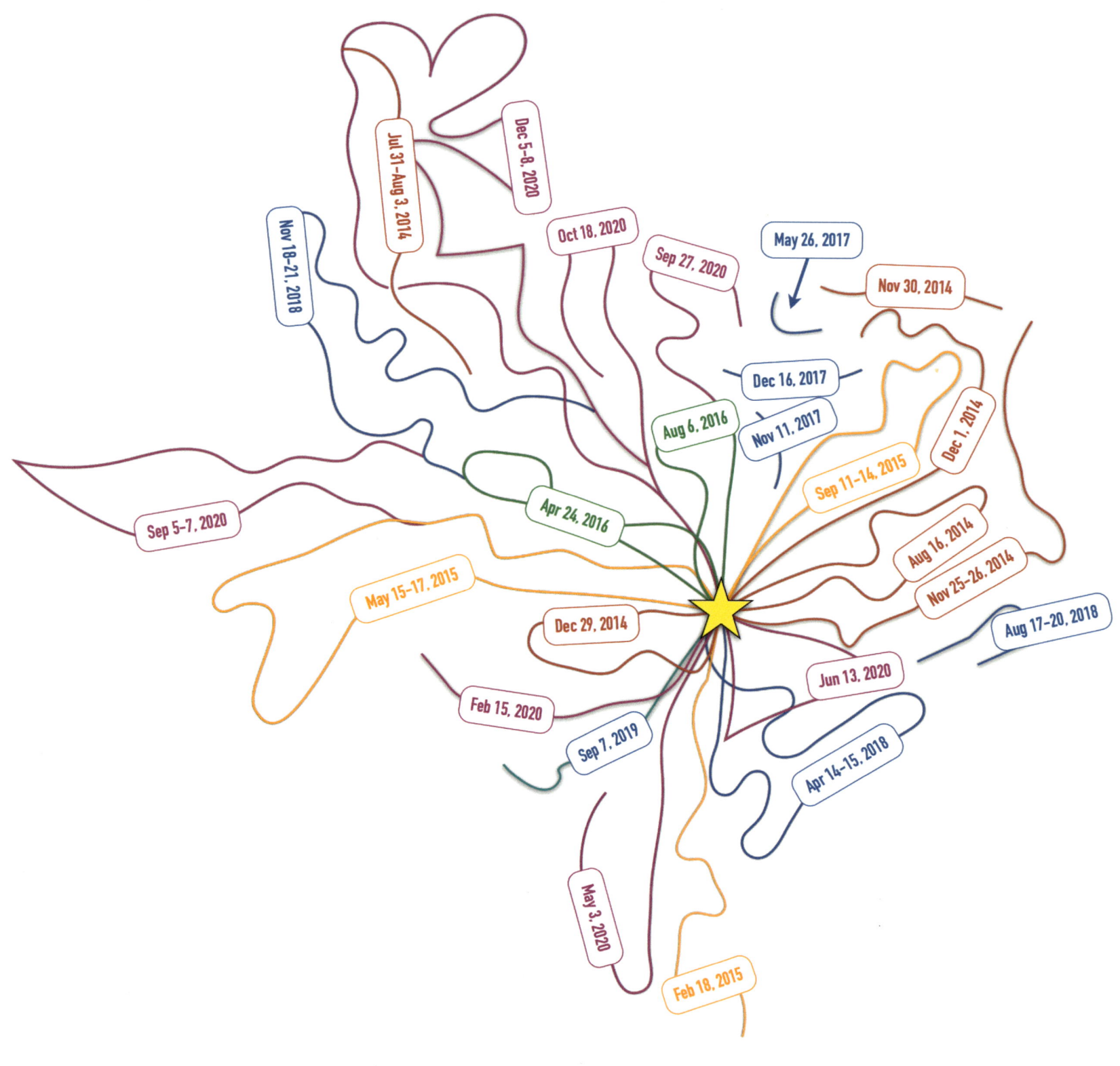

www.ingramcontent.com/pod-product-compliance
Lightning Source LLC
Chambersburg PA
CBHW040812120626

46547CB00004B/526